Dublin

Front cover: part of Dublin's Georgian heritage

Right: statue of James Joyce on North Earl Street

TOP 10 ATTRACTIONS

O'Connell Street • Dublin's grand boulevard, studded with monuments and statues, and the iconic General Post Office (page 60)

The Guinness Storehouse tour • Find out all about brewing and sample the freshest pint in town (page 45)

Kilmainham Gaol • Learn about life behind bars and what brought prisoners here (page 47)

The Custom House • One of Dublin's most elegant landmarks dominates the north bank of the Liffey (page 59)

Phoenix Park • The biggest urban park in Europe, with landscaped gardens, woods, pastures, various monuments and the zoo *(page 66)*

y College • Dublin's University has a string of famous ai and owns treasures such as the Book of Kells *(page 28)*

nal Gallery • Home to collection of works he 14th to the 20th ry *(page 53)*

Temple Bar • A network of narrow cobbled streets with lively bars and interesting markets *(page 37)*

n Castle • The centre lish rule in Ireland for centuries *(page 39)*

Christ Church • One of the city's two major cathedrals *(page 42)*, the other is **St Patrick's** *(page 49)*

CONTENTS

27

99
75

49

11

25

INTRODUCTION

Dublin is a fast-paced city hopping with great pubs and rich with history and culture. With a mix of Irish charm and European chic, it's a place that always seems to be changing before your very eyes. Cranes dot the skyline, particularly along the quays where construction continues apace, traffic is increasingly congested, and the city's frenetic rush hour couldn't be more at odds with the peaceful sway of the countryside. At night the streets are lively with revellers who pour into the city's pubs, bars, restaurants, clubs and cafes, and by day shoppers throng the popular shopping streets, department stores and shopping centres. Over a decade after the Celtic Tiger first began to roar, prosperity remains in the air of this energetic capital city.

The proverbial hospitality and warm welcome have not vanished in Dublin's increasing bustle, though the city's character is more complex than the souvenir shops suggest. Dublin sits on 1,000 years of history – and it is present everywhere, from the famous literary homes on Merrion Square to the bullet holes on the General Post Office (the paintings inside give a quick lesson). That history, along with a blooming economy has given birth to a new culture that has placed Dublin at the cutting-edge of Europe's arts, design and music scenes; an exciting development that merits leaving the pub behind for a while and seeing what the new Irish are all about.

Along the cobbled lanes of Temple Bar, rubbing shoulders with dozens of theme bars selling lurid green leprechauns and kitsch souvenirs, are galleries showing off dynamic artists and photographers whose talent looks to a world stage. Designers have made high fashion out of hand knits and tweeds.

Dublin City Hall

Musicians have proven you don't need a bodhrán to make it in Irish music. Boutiques sell sleek, Irish designed furnishings.

Prosperity has also brought with it a new emphasis on historic preservation. Dublin excels in packaging its past for the visitor. You can view artefacts from the Bronze Age, trace the history of the Easter Rising, or revisit Leopold Bloom's odyssey in *Ulysses*. Old buildings are used for modern purposes; for example, the 17th-century Royal Hospital at Kilmainham holds the Museum of Modern Art.

City on the Liffey

The River Liffey flows from west to east through the centre of the city to Dublin Bay and forms a natural line between the north and south sections of the city. Historically and culturally this north–south distinction has always been significant, and it still is today, with a dose of good-humoured rivalry between the two areas. 'I never go north of the Liffey,' one man remarked.

Further out, both north and south, are the sweeping curves of the Royal and Grand Canals. The occasional cry of gulls and unexpected distant vistas will remind you that Dublin is by the sea, and that the Wicklow Mountains, which hold Dublin closely to the coast, are within striking distance.

Dublin is an intimate city, physically small but tightly packed, a perfect place for walking. College Green, the home of Trinity College, provides a natural focus just south of O'Connell Bridge.

Lighting conditions

It won't rain on you in Dublin all the time. The climate here can best be described as 'changeable', and yet the sudden shifts from light to dark, sunshine to shower, are part of the city's magic. Buildings seem to transform themselves depending on the light; Dublin under a lowering sky is a different place from Dublin in sunshine.

O'Connell Street, the city's grand boulevard, leads north to Parnell Square and the Garden of Remembrance. To the south and east is St Stephen's Green and the best-preserved Georgian area, where the national museums are located. Along the south bank of the Liffey, to the west, is Temple Bar, up the hill from there are Dublin Castle and Christ Church Cathedral.

Enjoying Dublin

Literature has always flourished in Dublin, the only city to have produced three Nobel Prize for literature winners – Yeats, Shaw and Beckett. Joyce, the high

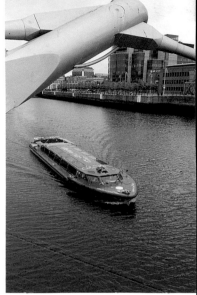

The Millennium Bridge over the Liffey

priest of literary Modernism, imagined and interpreted Dublin for the world in *Ulysses* (you'll see references to it everywhere). However, sometimes it seems that the city produced artists of this stature by accident, even against its will. Beckett and Joyce, among others, had to leave their homeland to understand it – and to be understood.

Dublin theatre is legendary, and no visitor should miss seeing a performance at the Abbey Theatre or Gate Theatre. The city's impact on the rock and pop music scene with the likes of U2 and Bob Geldof is well known – there's even a self-guided tour of their haunts. Traditional Irish music is alive and well, especially in the pubs, where you might easily walk in to a spontaneous live music 'session'. There has been a revival of storytelling, poetry reading and traditional dancing. And visual arts are finally coming into their own, showcased at the Museum of Modern Art in Kilmainham, and cutting-edge galleries.

Constantly crowded and busy, Grafton Street is the most visible centre for shopping, but retailers all over the city carry an international array of goods as well as the Irish crafts and souvenirs you expect. And while multinational chains have made inroads, the city is still packed with chic boutiques and colourful delis. Many shops, hotels and guesthouses have been owned and managed by the same families for years, and theirs is the welcome of traditional Dublin hospitality.

There was a time when you might have apologised for the range and quality of eateries in Dublin, but no longer. The city's food has undergone a metamorphosis, with international restaurants galore, and a new Irish cuisine that draws on Ireland's exceptional local produce including artisan cheeses and super-fresh seafood. Coffee has long replaced the once ubiquitous tea.

City and Countryside

In a city of such human proportions it is not surprising that parks and gardens abound, perfect for recreation and relaxation. Phoenix Park in the northwest is the largest city park in Europe, and is home to Dublin Zoo, but squares like St Stephen's Green are the garden oases of the city.

On the coast, Sandymount, Dollymount and Killiney strands are the places to go for a blast of fresh sea air. The atmospheric, brooding Wicklow Mountains and the Wicklow Mountains National Park provide a more rugged countryside, and the area has breathtaking houses and gardens such as Castletown, Mount Usher and Powerscourt. To the north and west are several historic sites: Malahide Castle, the evocative hill of Tara, and the long barrows of Knowth and Newgrange.

The DART (Dublin Area Rapid Transit) runs north and south along the coast. It's an ideal way for the visitor to reach outlying sights and villages. There are guided bus tours to sights outside the city.

Young at Heart?

Dublin is a young city. Almost half of Ireland's population is under 25, and with its universities and professional schools, Dublin also has a large student population. The universities attract students from all over the world, and this influx helps to make Dublin a busy, buzzing international city. And young graduates are not leaving now – multinational corporations and European Union investment mean there are plenty of opportunities for them at home. During the rise of the Celtic Tiger Dublin became a popular place to settle. So popular in fact that the Irish are actually beginning to come home.

Performing in a Temple Bar pub

A BRIEF HISTORY

Ireland has been inhabited since very ancient times, but Irish history really begins with the arrival of the Celts around the 6th century bc. They brought with them iron weapons, chariots and customs that quickly became dominant in the country. This period sparked myths and legends, later romanticised by Irish writers, that still exercise their power today.

The Celts were organised along a clan-based system, and Celtic Ireland became a series of independent kingdoms. These kingdoms acknowledged an elected High King, with his seat at fabled Tara, as overlord. There were no towns, and the cow was the medium of exchange. Learning was revered, games were played, and the poet was held in awe. Law and religion were important in Celtic culture. The religion was druidic, and the law was an elaborate written code, interpreted by a class of professional lawyers known as *brehons*. The *brehon* laws gave women a high status – they could own property, divorce, and even enter the professions.

Christianity and a Mission to Europe

St Patrick first came to Ireland as a prisoner, captured in an Irish raid on a Roman settlement in Britain. He eventually escaped, but returned to Ireland as a missionary in AD432. By the time of his death in 465, the whole country had been peacefully Christianised, which speaks for Patrick's natural diplomacy as well as his powers of persuasion. Many legends surround his mission. It was St Patrick who used the example of the shamrock to explain the Christian Trinity to King Laoghaire and an assembled crowd at Tara. The king was converted and the plant has been a symbol of Ireland ever since.

With Christianity and the sophisticated Celtic culture successfully fused, Ireland entered its 'Golden Age' (AD500 until around 800). The Irish monasteries became the major preserves of learning and literacy in the so-called 'Dark Ages'. Ireland was 'the light of the known world', sending its saints and scholars out all over Europe.

The Vikings Arrive

Throughout this period, Ireland's political organisation continued much as it had under pagan Celtic rule. There were still no towns; the site of Dublin was only a crossroads, known as *Baile Átha Cliath* ('Town of the Hurdles'; the Irish name is still seen on road signs and buses). From 795, Ireland was repeatedly raided by the Vikings. They sacked the great centres of learning and, in the 9th century, built a fort on the Liffey and founded Ireland's first town – *Dubh Linn* or 'Black Pool'. The remains of Viking fortifications can be seen today beneath Dublin Castle. The Vikings also introduced coinage and better ship-building techniques.

Medieval manuscript made during Ireland's Golden Age

In 988 the Irish kings finally united under the King of Munster, Brian Ború, and drove the Vikings north of the Liffey. After this defeat their influence waned, and they began to be absorbed into the general population. The Irish now held Dublin and in 1038 the first Christ Church Cathedral was founded.

English Rule Begins

In 1169 the Anglo-Normans landed in Wexford, beginning the struggle between England and Ireland that was to dominate Irish history until independence. The Norman incursion began with an internal power struggle. The king of Leinster invited Richard de Clare, known as 'Strongbow', to come to Ireland to help him reclaim his kingdom (Strongbow's tomb can be seen in Christ Church Cathedral). Successive waves of Anglo-Norman invaders followed Strongbow, bringing with them armour, the use of horses in battle, and the feudal system. Unlike the Irish, they favoured centralised administration, and enforced their rule with the building of fortified castles. In 1171 the English king, Henry II, came to Dublin. He granted a charter in 1174 that gave the city rights to free trade. By 1204 Dublin Castle was the centre of English administrative power in Ireland. The city elected its first mayor in 1229, and a parliament was held for the first time in 1297.

Dublin Castle, a mix of styles from down the ages

Beyond the Pale

The Anglo-Normans, following the pattern of earlier invaders, became rapidly assimilated, though the next two centuries were characterised by repeated attempts by the Irish to rid themselves of their overlords. They were very nearly successful: by the end of the 15th century England held only a small area around Dublin, walled off from the Norman inner city and known as the Pale, with the 'wild Irish' controlling all of the country outside.

All this changed under the Tudors. Henry VIII and Elizabeth I were determined to subdue Ireland, and sent in massive military expeditions. Henry VIII's break with Rome and the Dissolution of the Monasteries meant that by 1558 Dublin's two cathedrals, St Patrick's and Christ Church, had become Protestant (they remain so today). Elizabeth I founded Trinity College in Dublin as a seat of Protestant learning, and it remained just that well into the 20th century.

The Irish continued to resist, but the semi-independent kingdoms were never able to achieve real cohesion. By 1607, they were left leaderless by the 'Flight of the Earls'. The two Ulster earls, O'Neill and O'Donnell went into exile on the Continent, along with many other Irish lords.

From Cromwell to the Boyne

In 1649, Ireland's most hated conqueror, Oliver Cromwell, arrived in Dublin. His ruthless campaigns resulted in more than 600,000 Irish dead or deported. There was a massive dispossession of the Irish from their fertile lands in the east, and they were driven west of the Shannon; in Cromwell's phrase they could go to 'Hell or Connaught'. Some Irish still spit when they hear his name.

At the end of the century, when Catholic king James II came to the throne, the Irish felt they had no choice but to back him. James was defeated by William of Orange just north of Dublin at the Battle of the Boyne in 1690. As a result, the English parliament enacted the Penal Laws of 1704, which disenfranchised Catholics in order to keep the majority of Irish poor and powerless.

Wolfe Tone

Grattan and Wolfe Tone

The 18th century was not a good time for the native Irish, but the Protestant Ascendancy flourished. However, like others before them, they had come to identify themselves as Irish, and they were anxious to achieve at least a measure of self-government for Ireland. In 1782 an Irish parliament was formed in Dublin, largely through the energies of Henry Grattan, MP for the city. Grattan succeeded in having most of the Penal Laws repealed. But the independent parliament was short-lived – against Grattan's opposition, and through bribery and corruption, it voted to dissolve itself in 1800.

In the meantime, the influential ideas of the French Revolution were spreading. The United Irishmen, led by Wolfe Tone, was founded in 1791, a nonsectarian movement that sought the freedom of the Irish people, both Catholic and Protestant. Wolfe Tone secured aid from France, but a storm scattered the ships of the invading force. Tone was captured and either was murdered or committed suicide. He remains a revered figure in the Irish pantheon.

The Union and O'Connell

Under the Act of Union, Irish members of parliament now served in London. In 1803 there was yet another failed rebellion, led by the great Irish hero Robert Emmet. His speech from the dock and his horrendous execution have become the stuff of legend. Daniel O'Connell carried on the struggle. He formed the peaceful but powerful Catholic Association, and in 1829 the Duke of Wellington, in a bid to avoid a civil war, passed the Catholic Emancipation Bill, which allowed Irish Catholics to sit in the parliament at Westminster for the first time. O'Connell was made Lord Mayor of Dublin in 1841, but failed in his bid to have the Act of Union repealed and an Irish parliament re-established.

Famine and Home Rule

The Great Famine struck in 1845 with a blight on the staple food of the poor, the potato. It lasted until 1848, and it is estimated that more than one million people died and as many emigrated to escape the ravages of the catastrophe. By the end of the 1800s, Ireland's population was virtually halved. Ironically, there was plenty of food around – corn, cattle, sheep and flour – but it was not available to the poor.

In America a new organisation was formed, the Irish Republican Brotherhood, known as the Fenians. Their rebel-

Georgian Dublin

The Ascendancy in Dublin enjoyed an elegant lifestyle during this period. Theatre and music flourished. Dublin's importance grew dramatically as the city became the centre of social and business life in Ireland. Craftsmen and architects were imported from Europe and England to create public buildings such as the Custom House and the Four Courts; private mansions like Powerscourt and Leinster House; and Georgian squares like Merrion Square in south Dublin.

The glory of this lively and cosmopolitan city lasted until 1801, when the Act of Union brought Ireland under direct rule from London. Quite suddenly, everything came to a standstill: the rich and powerful left for England, and the city became a provincial capital in a state of long, slow decline.

lion was aborted, but the society remained active and was influential in the efforts of the National Land League, founded in 1879, which sought to change the tenant system. Charles Stewart Parnell, an Irish member of parliament, took up the cause, and the Land Acts, which enabled hard-pressed tenants to buy their land, were passed.

Parnell's other cause was the demand for Home Rule for Ireland. For a time, it looked as if the campaign was going to succeed, but political events, together with the citing of Parnell as co-respondent in a scandalous divorce case, led many to withdraw their support. The bill for Home Rule finally became law just as World War I broke out, but with the proviso that it was not to be enacted until hostilities ended.

The Fight for Freedom

Two years into the war, on Easter Monday, 24 April 1916, armed nationalists, led by trade unionist James Connolly and poet Padraig Pearse, took control of a number of key buildings in the capital. Pearse read out a Declaration of Independence from the General Post Office (GPO) on O'Connell Street. More than 500 people were killed and many buildings damaged – you can see the bullet holes on the GPO building and the Royal College of Surgeons – before the Easter Rising was put down. Fifteen of the leaders were executed, including Pearse and the wounded Connolly, who was brought to his execution in an ambulance and shot tied to a chair. The harshness of the British retribution galvanised the Irish – and in the words of Yeats's poem, 'All changed, changed utterly'. People were no longer content with the prospect of Home Rule – they wanted full independence.

In the general election of 1919 an overwhelming number of Sinn Féin ('Ourselves') republicans were returned to parliament. Instead of going to London, however, they set up a rebel parliament – the first Dáil Éireann – in Dublin, spark-

The British send in the tanks during the 1916 Easter Uprising

ing the War of Independence. This guerrilla conflict lasted until 1921, when a treaty was signed giving independence to all of Ireland, except for the six counties of Northern Ireland (where protestant support for the crown was overwhelming). Many republicans baulked at the prospect of only limited independence. Civil war broke out between the supporters of Michael Collins and Arthur Griffith, who had signed the treaty, and Éamon de Valera's followers who disagreed with the partitioning of the country. A year later, the war was over and the new Irish Free State was born.

Independence and After

In 1937, having made his way back into the Dáil at the head of a new party, de Valera created a republican constitution which took Ireland out of the British Commonwealth. The new republic elected its first president, Douglas Hyde, in 1938. During World War II, though bombs from German planes fell twice on Dublin, the country remained neutral. In 1948, the Irish Republic severed its last ties to Britain.

Neglect, conquest and isolation, however, had taken their toll, and at first independent Ireland was characterised by continued poverty and emigration, a parochial approach to affairs, and domination by the Church. However, things were about to start looking up: Ireland received huge financial assistance from the European Community, which it joined in 1972, and by the 1990s the economy was beginning to show signs of a boom. The arts began to blossom too. In 1991, Dublin was designated European City of Culture. Musicians such as U2 and Sinead O'Connor put Dublin on the world stage, as did film makers such as Neil Jordan *(The Crying Game)* and Alan Parker *(The Commitments)*.

The Irish flag flying over the GPO

Ireland has developed into an altogether more forward looking, confident society. In 1990, the dynamic Mary Robinson was chosen as its first woman president. Debates on such issues as divorce and abortion followed, preparing the country for the challenges of the 21st century. In 2002, Ireland was one of the first twelve nations to adopt the euro. As capital of a prosperous economy today, this forward-looking, self-assured Dublin is now very much a European city.

Historical Landmarks

8000BC First evidence of human habitation in Ireland.

AD432 St Patrick brings Christianity to Ireland.

AD795 The Vikings arrive, later building a fort on the Liffey called *Dubh Linn*.

1014 BrianBorú defeats the Vikings at the Battle of Clontarf.

1038 Christ Church established.

1171 Henry II lands at Dublin and claims feudal lordship.

1204 Anglo-Normans rule from Dublin Castle.

1297 First parliamentary sessions in Dublin.

1534 Henry VIII suppresses Catholic Church.

1592 Founding of Trinity College by Elizabeth I.

1649 Oliver Cromwell invades Ireland and devastates the country.

1690 Supporters of Catholic James II defeated at the Battle of the Boyne.

1791 Wolfe Tone's rebellion.

1800 The Irish Parliament is forced to dissolve itself.

1803 Robert Emmet's rebellion and execution.

1829 Daniel O'Connell secures passage of the Catholic Emancipation Act.

1845 Ireland's Great Famine strikes, and lasts until 1848.

1904 Abbey Theatre founded.

1916 The Easter Rising.

1919 Sinn Féin becomes the first Dáil and declares Irish independence.

1919–21 Ireland at war with Britain.

1922 Outbreak of Irish Civil War.

1927 First general election.

1937 Irish constitution adopted.

1939–45 City bombed by Germany; Ireland remains neutral.

1948 The Republic of Ireland Act severs the last links with Britain.

1972 Ireland joins the European Economic Community.

1990 Ireland elects its first woman president, Mary Robinson.

1991 Dublin elected European City of Culture.

2002 The euro introduced as Ireland's new unit of currency.

2006 The government launches a 20-year strategy to create a bilingual, Irish and English-speaking society.

WHERE TO GO

Dublin is a compact city, and many of its important sites are within easy walking distance of one another. There are also bus services and the Luas tram system that will take you to attractions away from the city centre. You can get information from the Dublin Bus Office in Upper O'Connell Street or from the Dublin Tourism (see below). The DART (suburban railway) travels north and south along the coast, a pleasant scenic ride. Car rental is quite expensive, and, with congested traffic and parking problems, is not a good choice within the city.

Your first port of call should be **Dublin Tourism** (open Mon–Sat 9am–5.30pm, until 7pm July-Aug, Sun 10.30am–3pm; <www.visitdublin.com>), housed in the former St Andrew's Church in Suffolk Street; there is also an office in O'Connell Street. You'll find maps, leaflets and other useful information there, and you can also use the service to arrange accommodation and book tours, theatre tickets and other entertainment. In addition, Dublin Tourism has devised and signposted three walking tours, which you can follow using the booklets provided. Another good orientation exercise is to start with an organised sightseeing tour with Dublin Bus from Upper O'Connell Street or Bus Éireann from the Travel Centre at Busáras in Store Street.

Left: the Spire of Dublin, O'Connell Street

The Dublin Pass

Some museums are closed on Monday, and opening hours tend to be restricted during the winter months. The national museums have free admission, but the Dublin Pass, available online and from the tourist offices, gives you free entry or guided tours to over 30 major attractions and museums. Log onto <www.dublinpass.ie> for more information.

Grafton Street

AROUND GRAFTON STREET

Grafton Street, south of the river, is Dublin's main shopping street. This central pedestrian thoroughfare, enlivened by street entertainers, is lined with stores including the famous Brown Thomas department store, Laura Ashley and Marks and Spencer. The original **Bewley's Oriental Café**, a city landmark for over a century, has been revamped into a popular breakfast spot, along with a lunchtime café-theatre, a café-bar-deli upstairs and an elegant but casual fish restaurant called Mackerel. Stop by to see the café's distinctive art deco features, including the rear stained-glass windows by Harry Clarke. On the alley alongside is **St Teresa's Church**, with stained-glass windows by Phyllis Burke and a fine sculpture by John Hogan.

A number of interesting shopping complexes are set around Grafton Street. The smart **Powerscourt Townhouse Centre** is probably the most notable of these (a sign points the way just beyond Bewley's to the Clarendon Street entrance). This 1770s mansion was formerly the residence of Viscount Powerscourt and still possesses some magnificent plasterwork, particularly in the rear exit hall. The old house has been tastefully converted, with a pleasant glass-roofed central courtyard surrounded by balconies. There are many cafés and restaurants, and you can shop on the various levels for antiques, crafts and Irish and International designer clothes. At the top is an art gallery with changing exhibitions. In summer there is a programme of lunchtime recitals.

Next to the shopping centre, the **Dublin Civic Museum** at 58 South William is currently closed. Most of the museum's exhibits on the history of the city are in storage, but its main artefact – the head from Nelson's Pillar that once rose above O'Connell Street, until it was blown up by the IRA in 1966 – is now on display at the **Dublin City Library and Archive** (138–144 Pearse Street, open Mon–Thur 10am–8pm and Fri–Sat 10am–5pm).

Opposite the historical facade of Powerscourt Centre a pedestrian street, Castle Market, leads to another historical shopping area. The **George's Street Arcade** is a bustling market selling clothes, food and trinkets and includes an assortment of traditional cafés and coffee shops, all housed under 18th-century warehouse arches. At the other end of the arcade is South Great George's Street, which has more one-off shops and the lovely Victorian Long Hall pub, an atmospheric watering hole with wood-and-glass interior decoration.

At the top end of Grafton Street, where it meets Nassau Street, you will see Jean Rynhart's **statue of Molly Malone**, subject of the well-known 18th-century ballad, with her barrow and a very low décolletage. Erected in 1988 to celebrate Dublin's millennium, it has become known to irreverent locals as the 'Tart with the Cart'.

Molly Malone – the 'Tart with the Cart'

Down the street from Molly is the **Bank of Ireland** (guided tours Tues 10.30am, 11.30am and 1.45pm; chamber open Mon–Fri 10am–4pm, until 5pm Thur). Constructed in 1729 to house the Irish Parliament, the striking building preserves the impressive chamber of the Irish House of Lords with its 18th-century tapestries and coffered ceiling. The building is really a series of additions to an original structure, although the overall effect is one of elegance and superb proportion. The Corinthian portico was designed by James Gandon, who was also responsible for many fine buildings in Georgian Dublin, including the Custom House on the north bank of the Liffey. Plans to house parliament here after Independence came to nothing; Leinster House in Kildare Street was chosen instead.

Behind the bank in Foster Place is the intimate **Bank of Ireland Arts Centre** (open Tues–Fri 9.30am–4pm, tour times 10am, 11am and 3pm; admission charge). Upstairs is an exhibit on the history of banking and the short-lived Irish Parliament. The centre presents free lunchtime concerts, poetry readings, art exhibitions and various other cultural activities.

Trinity College

Across College Street is **Trinity College** (<www.tcd.ie>), founded by Elizabeth I in 1592 to educate the Protestant Anglo-Irish Ascendancy. Only in 1970 did the Catholic Church lift its boycott of the university and proclaim that it was no longer a mortal sin for a Catholic to attend the Protestant university. Today the college is one of the geographical and social hubs of the city, attracting students from around the world. Famous graduates include Jonathan Swift, Oliver Goldsmith, Bram Stoker, Oscar Wilde and Samuel Beckett; resistance heroes Robert Emmet and Wolfe Tone also studied here.

The university sits on College Green, an island of magnificent buildings, open squares and green spaces, surrounded by a sea of traffic. Walk through the gates of the west front, designed by Theodore Jacobsen and built in 1752. The statues on either side are of Edmund Burke and Oliver Goldsmith. You are welcome to explore College Green, but some of the buildings may be closed, depending on the time of year. A good way to do this is to join one of the student-led **walking tours** around the campus, where you'll learn about the history of the college and the buildings, and hear some amusing anecdotes about its most famous graduates. The tours run from mid-April until early October and leave from inside the west front gate, every 40 minutes from 10.15am.

The imposing Campanile at Trinity College

Front Square and **Parliament Square**, dating from the 18th century, are surrounded by the Chapel, Dining Hall, Examination Hall and 1937 Reading Room, and anchored by the splendid Campanile. On your left the **Dining Hall**, designed by Richard Castle, has been falling down ever since it was finished in the 1740s and has undergone frequent rebuilding. It was beautifully restored after a damaging fire in 1984. The late 18th-century **Chapel** displays some fine plasterwork and dazzling stained-glass windows, together with a 20th-century organ in an 18th-century case. Opposite the Chapel is the **Examination Hall**, where concerts are given occasionally; otherwise it is rarely open to the public (look through the spy hole in the door). The beautiful stucco ceiling is by Michael Stapleton, who is also responsible for the ceilings in the Dublin Writers Museum.

Among the paintings is a portrait of Archbishop James Usher, who donated the Book of Kells *(see below)* to the University Library. Both the Chapel and Examination Hall were designed by Sir William Chambers, the architect responsible for Casino, Marino *(see page 76)*.

The 30-m (100-ft) high **Campanile**, built in 1853 by Sir Charles Lanyon, houses the university's bells. It is impossible to miss the huge *Reclining Connected Forms* by Henry Moore in **Library Square**, or Alexander Calder's *Cactus* behind the Old Library in **Fellows Square**. Architect Paul Koralek's 1967 **Berkeley Library**, fronted by Arnaldo Pomodoro's *Sphere Within Sphere*, fits seamlessly into the earlier buildings. The eastern side of the square once housed Oliver Goldsmith's rooms; renovated in Victorian times, little of the original building remains.

Trinity's most important possession is the 9th-century **Book of Kells**. This ornate text containing the four Gospels is said to be the finest illustrated medieval manuscript in the world. The exhibition, 'Turning Darkness into Light' (open Mon–Sat 9.30am–5pm; Sun Oct–Apr noon–4.30pm, May–Sept 9.30am–4.30pm; admission charge), is in the **Colonnades** beneath the Old Library. It begins with a series of panels explaining how such medieval works were created. The book itself is displayed along with other illuminated manuscripts such as the Book of Durrow or the Book of

All-in ticket

The Book of Kells admission ticket also includes entry to the Long Room and other library exhibitions. Entry tickets can be purchased at a reduced rate if bought in conjunction with a student-led guided tour of the campus *(see page 27)*.

Trinity College Old Library

Armagh; pages of the books are turned every six weeks. The exhibition is tremendously popular, so be prepared for some long queues at the entrance.

Upstairs is the impressive **Long Room**, or Old Library, which opened in 1732. A barrel-ceilinged chamber 64m (209ft) long, with windows along both sides, it holds Trinity's oldest books, including a Shakespeare folio.

Across Fellows' Square in the modern Arts Building is the airy **Douglas Hyde Gallery** (open Mon–Fri 11am–6pm, Thur until 7pm; Sat 11am–4.45pm; free; <www.douglashyde gallery.com>), a modern two level exhibition space and the place to go for cutting edge Irish and international art.

The Samuel Beckett Theatre and the Players Theatre provide budding students with a stage on which to shine. Both are located in the **Samuel Beckett Centre** (<www.tcd.ie/drama>) and produce an array of student productions with the occasional touring show.

If you'd like to see college life in action – and the weather's good – make your way to the **Pavillion** on College Park, at the opposite end of campus to the main gates. It serves student-priced drinks and is surrounded by green spaces that sprout many a sunning student on a warm day. It's a great place to relax, watch the rugby team practice and hear others fret over upcoming exams. If the weather's cold, try the **Buttery** under the Dining Hall building – an eatery and bar in the basement that's low on comfort, but full of high jinx.

Dawson and Kildare Streets

From College Green head down Nassau Street (site of many craft and souvenir shops), then turn right into Dawson Street. Here you'll find bookshops, boutiques and another shopping complex, this one built on the site of the Royal Hibernian Hotel and naturally called the **Royal Hibernian Way**.

Leinster House, seat of Ireland's Parliament

St Anne's Church (facing Anne Street South) has some colourful stained glass, and is a popular venue for daytime concerts. A few doors down is the charming **Mansion House**, residence of the mayor of Dublin since 1715. The house was built in 1710 for a property speculator, one Joshua Dawson, after whom the street was named. Behind it is the **Round Room**, where in 1919 the Irish parliament adopted the Declaration of Independence.

Turn down Molesworth Street, lined with several fine-art galleries, to reach Kildare Street, where you will see the elegant entrance to **Leinster House**, once owned by the earls of Kildare, and now home to the Irish parliament. This building is believed by some to have provided the basis for the US White House, which was designed by Irish architect James Hoban in 1870. It is open to the public when parliament is not sitting. On one side of the building is the **National Library** (<www.nli.ie>), on the other is a branch of the National Museum *(see below)*. Tickets are required for the library reading room and are available at the information desk. Over half a million items here provide a vast archive of the nation. Exhibitions are often held in the splendid entrance hall.

The Museum of Archaeology and History located on Kildare Street is just one of four branches belonging to the **National Museum**, Dublin's most important historic collection. The other branches include the nearby Museum of Natural History; Collins Barracks near Phoenix Park, which is linked by a free bus service; and the Museum of Country Life in Castlebar, in County Mayo. All are free and found on the museum's website (<www.museum.ie>).

The **Museum of Archaeology and History** (open Tues–Sat 10am–5pm, Sun 2–5pm, closed Mon; guided tours take 40 minutes and depart regularly) contains Bronze-Age Irish gold and other archaeological finds. Opened in 1890, the building itself is noteworthy for its entrance hall and Rotunda, mosaic floors and the elaborate blue-and-yellow majolica decoration on the pediments and jambs of the doors. The exhibits are state-of-the art. **Ór: Ireland's Gold** displays the astonishing accomplishments of goldsmiths from 2000 to 700BC. Medieval treasures include the famous Ardagh Chalice and Tara Brooch, along with metalwork from the Viking period. The museum also has a small Egyptian gallery and an exhibit focusing on the history of Irish independence. There is also a good, but crowded café and a small gift shop.

Deane & Woodward, the architects responsible for the library and museum, also built the Kildare Street Club, in 1861. This marvellous Victorian-Gothic building is famous for the fanciful stone carvings around the base of its pillars (one pillar, reputedly depicting the club members, shows monkeys playing billiards). The club itself was a bastion of Ascendancy establishment. The building now houses the

Finding Your Ancestors

If you have an Irish last name or Irish ancestry, you may want to join the crowd that comes to Ireland ancestor hunting. Your grandmother's family stories may be the clue – begin at home by collecting family names.

Dublin is a good place to start your search. The National Library in Kildare Street has a genealogical department on the first floor which has a large collection of genealogical and historical records and provides a free advisory service. Other sources are the Office of the Registrar General in the Custom House, with records of Protestant marriages, births and deaths going back to 1845 and Catholic records from 1861; the Record Office of the Four Courts; and the Registry of the Deeds, in Henrietta Street. If you know the county your family came from, or better still, the town or village, you can go directly to the appropriate parish registers; these go back more than 200 years. Churchyard monuments and gravestones can also be a source of information.

Heraldic Museum and Genealogical Office (open Mon–Wed 10am–8.30pm, Thur–Fri 10am–4.30pm, Sat 10am–12.30pm; free), with exhibits on the history of heraldry. Although the office of Ireland's Chief Herald does not undertake genealogical research for visitors, if you qualify and have the requisite cash to spare, you can apply for a Grant of Arms. Opposite this bastion of Irish heritage is **Café Una**, the only Irish speaking café/restaurant in Dublin with traditional Irish dishes and contemporary European cuisine. It's more bi-lingual than exclusively Irish-speaking, though, so don't panic if your Gaelic isn't up to much!

St Stephen's Green

Walk to the bottom of Kildare Street and you will reach **St Stephen's Green**, a 9-hectare (22-acre) park in the heart of the city, surrounded by some beautiful buildings. Although formally laid out as a public park only in 1877–80, it is the oldest green in Dublin, dating back to medieval times. A popular and often crowded place, the Green contains large formal lawns with ornate gardens, duck ponds, a bandstand and a children's playground.

Entering the park from St Stephen's Green North you will come across the **Wolfe Tone Memorial** opposite the famous Shelbourne Hotel (1824), and behind it a work entitled *Famine*, both by sculptor Edward Delaney. The **Three Fates** fountain is a monument to the Irish spirit. Presented by Germany in thanks to the Irish who opened their country to

Bust of James Joyce at St Stephen's Green

orphaned German children after World War II, the three forlorn figures face Earlsfort Terrace, twisting a piece of string representing fate. Facing St Stephen's Green South is Marjorie Fitzgibbon's bust of **James Joyce**. Working your way around the park, you will see the 1907 **Fusilier's Arch** at the Grafton Street corner.

The **St Stephen's Green Shopping Centre** at the south end of Grafton Street, a pseudo-Victorian iron-and-glass structure, was built in the 1980s, and is known locally as 'The Wedding Cake'. It houses a wide selection of shops as well as a café-restaurant on the top floor, under the glass dome.

Halfway down the west side of the green is the massive Georgian **Royal College of Surgeons**, built in 1806. Those chips in the stonework are bullet holes from the 1916 Easter Rising – the building was occupied by independence fighters led by Countess Markievicz.

Gardeners tending the Green

One of Dublin's best-kept secrets is the **Iveagh Gardens**, accessible from Clonmel Street via Harcourt Street or from behind the National Concert Hall off Earlsfort Terrace. Neither entrance is obvious, hence the gardens' sense of seclusion. Designed as a series of pleasure gardens in the Italianate style in 1863, with cascades, spectacular fountains, and rustic grottoes, the gardens were opened to the public in 1991.

The Georgian curve of Harcourt Street (constructed in 1775) was once home to George Bernard Shaw (Nos 60–61). The **Shaw Birthplace Museum** at 33 Synge Street (open May– Sept Mon–Tues and Thur–Fri 10am–1pm and 2–5pm, Sat–Sun 2–5pm; admission charge), is marked by a plaque written by the great man himself. This Victorian house where he spent his early years has exhibits on Shaw and the Dublin he knew. It is furnished as a small but charming Dublin household typical of the period. Tours and booklets are available in a number of languages, and the staff are very friendly.

From here it is a short walk, following the signs, to the small **Irish-Jewish Museum** (open May–Sept Tues, Thur and Sun 11am–3.30pm; Oct–Apr Sun only 10.30am–2.30pm; free) in Walworth Road. This former synagogue, set in the heart of what was the city's Jewish quarter in the late 19th/early 20th century, tells the story of the Jews in Ireland by means of documents, memorabilia and old photographs, revealing a little-known part of Dublin's community. (Look for a Guinness bottle with a Hebrew label.)

Back along the south side of St Stephen's Green begins a fine array of buildings. The first of these is the **University Church**, built in 1853 by Cardinal Henry Newman, then rector of University College Dublin (UCD). The strangely compelling Byzantine-style interior is a very popular venue for weddings. Next door, Nos 85 and 86 comprise the exquisite **Newman House**, part of University College (guided tours

The Newman House contains rococo busts of man and beast

June–Aug Tues–Fri tours at noon, 2, 3 and 4pm; admission charge). Number 85 dates from 1740 and contains the famous Apollo Room, which has panels depicting Apollo and the muses, and the magnificent rococo salon, both by the La Francini brothers, who also worked on Russborough House *(see page 73)*. Number 86 next door, which is largely the work of Robert West, has even more elaborate ornamentation.

James Joyce was a student here, and, towards the end of his life, the poet Gerard Manley Hopkins lectured here. One of the classrooms Joyce attended can be seen on the guided tour, and Hopkins's room has been restored. There is a very pleasant terrace and in the basement is The Commons, which ranks among the best restaurants in Dublin.

Just beyond Newman House is **Iveagh House**, home to the Irish government's Department of Foreign Affairs, but closed to the public. Both Newman House and Iveagh House were designed by Richard Castle.

Beyond Iveagh House in Earlsfort Terrace (turn south) is the **National Concert Hall**, of impressive proportions and uncertain acoustics – it's a conversion of an old Examination Hall of University College.

Back at the northeast corner of St Stephen's Green, near the Shelbourne Hotel, you can turn right into Merrion Row to peer through the railings at the small **Huguenot Cemetery** (no entry to visitors). The cemetery dates back to 1693, when French Protestants, fleeing persecution in their native land, settled in Dublin, bringing with them their architectural and weaving skills, which greatly enriched their adopted city.

At the end of Ely Place, which runs south from Merrion Row and Baggot Street, is the **Royal Hibernian Academy** (open Tues–Sat 11am–5pm, Thur until 8pm, Sun 2–5pm; <www.royalhibernaianacademy.com>), where temporary contemporary art shows are held.

OLD DUBLIN

West of O'Connell Street, around Christ Church Cathedral, is the site of the original Viking town of *Dubh Linn*, which developed eastwards along the river towards Trinity College. In 1592, when Trinity was built, it was not in but near Dublin.

Temple Bar

Between the river and Dame Street is **Temple Bar**, once a run down area but now a firm fixture on the tourist map, famous for its nightlife and streetlife. Along the narrow cobbled lanes dating from the 18th century – partly pedestrianised and fairly free of traffic – you will find some original architecture, and many lively pubs, clubs, cafés, alternative shops and restaurants. Temple Bar is also home to a wealth of artists and musicians, and there are crafts and art workshops, galleries and music centres.

You can enter Temple Bar from Dame Street, or from Fleet Street (off Westmoreland Street), or you can walk through **Merchants Arch**, opposite the picturesque arching Ha'penny Bridge, into Temple Bar Square. Continuing along Temple Bar, you'll come to Eustace Street and Meeting House Square. Most of the cultural centres that make Temple Bar interesting are located in this area. The **Irish Film Centre** *(see page 94)* in Eustace Street opened in 1992 and is the main outlet for art-house and foreign films. It maintains a popular café/bar and its shop has a good selection of posters and books on film theory. Also in Eustace Street is an information office and a cultural centre for children, **The Ark** *(see page 96)*.

On Meeting House Square is the **Gallery of Photography** (open Tues–Sat 11am–6pm, Sun 1–6pm; free; <www.gallery ofphotography.ie>), displaying photographs of Dublin past and present alongside changing exhibitions of Irish and international photography. There are also books and posters for sale. The **National Photographic Archive** (open Mon–Fri 10am–5pm, Sat 10am–2pm, exhibition area only; free), also located on Meeting House Square, maintains the photographic collections of the National Library of Ireland. There are reading rooms for research and temporary exhibitions.

On Curved Street, the **Temple Bar Music Centre** is a resource centre for music, media and stage production *(see page 93)*. The **Project Arts Centre** (39 East Essex Street) displays avant-garde painting and sculpture and also has a performance space upstairs.

On Dame Street, Temple Bar's southern boundary, is a gem of Victorian architecture: the **Olympia Theatre** *(see page 93)*. Built in 1870, its canopy of stained glass and cast iron is the oldest in Dublin; its enthusiastic interior decoration is also typical of the era. The restored theatre has a regular schedule of lighthearted plays and concerts. Just across the way is **City Hall**, built originally as the Royal

At the heart of Temple Bar

Exchange in 1769–79. This fine building with its Corinthian portico was designed by Thomas Cooley. The **Story of the Capital** (open Mon–Sat 10am–5.15pm, Sun 2–5pm; admission charge; guided tours of City Hall also available) traces the history of Dublin over the last 1,000 years). Just to the west of City Hall lies one of Dublin's most important historic sites, Dublin Castle.

Dublin Castle

Today, as you walk through the Great Gate into the spacious Georgian yard, **Dublin Castle** (guided tours Mon–Fri 10am–4.45pm, Sat–Sun 2–4.45pm; admission charge) looks both serene and imposing. For seven centuries the real and symbolic centre of British military and social power, it is a monument that still has resonance for Dubliners. The castle has been built and rebuilt several times over the course of its history, and little remains of the original Anglo-Norman structure that was built in 1204. It sits on the site of the *Dubh Linn* (Black Pool) that gave Dublin its name.

The guided tour commences with the **State Apartments** on the south side of the building. Lavishly furnished and decorated, with much original period furniture, the rooms are used for ceremonial events, visits from foreign dignitaries, and EU meetings. The **Connolly Room** is so called because it was here that the wounded James Connolly spent his last night before being executed for his part in the Easter Rising. You may notice the exquisite ceiling in the **Granard Room**. It was moved here from Mespil House and is called the 'Hibernia Ceiling'. The **Drawing Room** was partially destroyed by fire in 1941, and its furnishings are faithful reproductions; the huge (repaired) Ming punch bowl is particularly striking.

Taking a break outside Dublin Castle

A splendid carpet, with a design based on a page from the Book of Kells *(see page 28)*, covers the floor of the **Throne Room**. The rather large throne was last used in 1911 by George V. In the lovely **Picture Gallery**, convex wall mirrors made it possible for the host at table to keep his eye on everyone, particularly the servants. The enormous **St Patrick's Hall**, with its painted ceiling by Vincenzo Valdre, contains the banners and coats of arms of the now-defunct Knights of St Patrick. The hall is now used for the inauguration of the Irish president.

One of the most interesting parts of the tour is the excavation of the **Viking and Norman Defences**. Visitors can stand in the dry bed of the old moat, traverse imaginative gangways over the encroaching river (the Poddle, not the Liffey), and view the stairs at which boats once landed provisions for the castle. In the restored **Treasury**

Castle sculpture

(built in 1715, located in the Lower Yard), browse in the bookshop or relax in the Castle Vaults Bistro and Patisserie.

The oldest remaining part of the castle is the **Record Tower** (1258), visible as you leave the upper yard. The Gothic-revival 19th-century **Church of the Most Holy Trinity**, adjacent to the tower, has stone work by Edward Smyth and a fan-vaulted ceiling. The Crypt Arts Centre is under the church and presents exhibitions, plays and concerts.

The Legend of British Justice

Above the main gate of Dublin Castle stands a statue of Justice. The fact that it has its back turned to the city was seen by Dubliners as an apt symbol of British rule. The farce doesn't end there though. This Justice, thanks to the naivety of the sculptor, has no blindfold. Furthermore the statue, inadvertantly of course, drained rainwater from the head, down the arm and into the the metal scales she holds, tipping them out of balance.

A modern addition to the castle precinct is the **Chester Beatty Library** (open May–Sept Mon–Fri 10am–5pm, Sat 11am–5pm, Sun 1–5pm; Oct–Apr closed Mon; free), which moved here from Ballsbridge. It is a treasure house of Islamic manuscripts, Chinese, Japanese and Indian art and texts. Biblical papyri and Christian manuscripts are also on display, completing one of the richest collections of the written word in Western and Eastern cultures. The library itself includes copies of the Koran and codices dating from the second century BC. This superb collection won the European Museum of the Year award in 2002.

Christ Church Cathedral and Environs

Further up the hill on Castle Street from the Great Gate is the first of Dublin's two major cathedrals, **Christ Church Cathedral** in Christchurch Place (June–Aug daily from 9am–6pm; Sept–May daily 9.45–6pm; admission charge). Standing, like the castle, on a hill, the cathedral rises on the site of King Sitric's 11th-century wooden church. The foundations date back to 1172 when Strongbow, the Earl of Pembroke, had it rebuilt as a stone structure. By 1558, after Henry VIII's break with the Roman Catholic Church, all the existing foundations in Dublin had become Anglican (see page 15).

Unfortunately, the church building was massively and unsympathetically restored in 1871–8, when most of the original interior was ripped out. However, there is still much to appreciate in Christ Church, including the impressive stonework, soaring nave, and the handsome 19th-century encaustic floor tiles based on a 13th-century pattern. Strongbow's tomb is in the church; and in the **Peace Chapel** is a somewhat macabre artefact – the embalmed heart of St Lawrence O'Toole, the influential 12th-century archbishop of Dublin, which is kept in a cage suspended on the wall near the altar. The cathedral choir traces its origins back to 1480 and has the distinction of taking part in the world's first ever performance of Handel's Messiah. Choral Evensong is on Wednesdays and Thursdays at 6pm.

The vast, vaulted medieval crypt is the oldest structure in Dublin. An exhibition, entitled **Treasures of Christ Church**, takes up much of the crypt. An additional charge is required to see this limited number of ancient texts, plus the tabernacle of James II, a William of Orange plate, commemorating his victory in the Battle of the Boyne, and a 1666 Common Prayer Book. In the open areas of the crypt, amongst the forest of heavy stone pillars are a few items of note, including stocks dating from 1670, medieval carved stones and a curious exhibit – a mummified cat and a rat, found trapped in the organ pipes.

In the Old Synod Hall, just across the road from the cathedral (and linked to it by a bridge), you will find **Dublinia** (open Apr–Sept daily 10am–5pm; Oct–Mar Mon–Fri 11am–4pm,

Christ Church Cathedral

Welcome to Dublinia!

Sat– Sun 10am–4pm; admission charge), a sight-and-sound re-creation (in five languages) of Dublin in medieval times. You can walk through the streets of the old city, experience a medieval market and visit a Merchant's House. Upstairs is a gift shop and the entrance to the connecting walkway to the cathedral; you can climb the tower, which has an interesting view of the surroundings.

Wood Quay, on the south bank of the river (downhill from the arch and dominated by the featureless offices of the Dublin Corporation) is the site of the original Viking settlement. Unfortunately, the construction of these offices obliterated much of the archaeological dig that unearthed the original layout of the 9th-century quay, but the artefacts that were found are on view in the National Museum *(see page 31)*.

A short distance from the cathedral on High Street are the two **St Audoen's churches**. The restored Church of Ireland St Audoen's is the older of the two (*circa* 1190) and is the only remaining medieval church in the city (interior access June–Sept Mon–Wed 9.30am–4.45pm). Next door is the narrow, lofty neoclassical facade of Catholic St Audoen's, built in 1847. Both churches stand beside what remains of the old city walls, and St Audoen's is the only surviving gate. In medieval times the High Cross of the Norman city, where decrees and notices of excommunication were read out, stood on the High Street. Granite markers erected in 1991 indicate the line of the old city walls.

West from here in Thomas Street, a plaque on the decommissioned and forlorn-looking **St Catherine's Church** (built in 1769) marks the spot where the famed Irish resistance hero Robert Emmet was hanged in 1803. **John's Lane Church** further down Thomas Street is more remarkable. Though just over 100 years old, it is one of the most attractive churches in the city. Thomas Street West becomes James's Street, where the **Guinness Brewery** has been situated ever since 1759.

Guinness Brewery and Beyond

Well west of the city centre lie several of Dublin's top tourist attractions. Handily, they are all clustered near Heuston Station, which is well serviced by bus and tram from the centre. The **Guinness Storehouse** (open daily 9.30am–5pm, until 7pm July–Aug; admission charge; <www.guinness-storehouse. com>) is the latest incarnation of the Guinness Brewery tour

Going with the flow at the Guinness Storehouse

Enjoying the view of Dublin from the Gravity bar

– and an ultra-modern one at that. This self-guided tour begins on the ground level with ingredients and ends in the very stylish **Gravity bar** atop the brewery with a 360-degree view of Dublin and the freshest (and free-est) pint of Guinness in town. Along the way you get to see and sniff the various stages of the brewing process. Despite all the entertaining technology, the tour is ultimately educational, as you watch films of old coopers making the casks for the brew and learn just how Guinness is created from the four simple ingredients of water, barley, hops and yeast.

The restored Royal Hospital at Kilmainham, which now houses the **Irish Museum of Modern Art** (open Tues–Sat 10am–5.30pm, Sun noon–5.30pm, Thur 10am–8pm July and August, closed Mon; free; <www.modernart.ie>) is Dublin's most important 17th-century building (1684) and is worth a visit for its own sake. With its wonderful light and space, it makes a tremendous exhibition area. The museum's holdings include the Gordon Lambert Collection, with more than 100 works dating from the 1960s–70s. The real attractions, however, are the numerous temporary exhibits that the museum hosts. There is an international residency programme for artists, and visitors may meet the artists in their studios (depending on schedules). Concerts and special events are also held in the museum, and there is an atmospheric café in the vaults.

Further west is the evocative museum of the **Kilmainham Gaol** (open Apr–Sept daily 9.30am–6pm; Oct–Mar daily 9.30am–5.30pm; admission charge). Kilmainham was the major Irish prison for well over a century, with Éamon de Valera as its last prisoner in 1924. An excellent exhibition traces the history of the prison (including a section on Victorian theories about prisons and the treatment of prisoners), as well as the political and social events that brought many of the prisoners here. A 25-minute audio-visual presentation in the prison chapel is followed by a guided tour through the dark corridors of the 18th-century part of the building, where you can see the cells occupied by the condemned leaders of the Easter Rising – they were executed in the prison yard.

A tour of Kilmainham Gaol

Nearby, on the south bank of the Liffey opposite Phoenix Park, is the **Irish National War Memorial Park**. Created in the 1930s to designs by the architect and landscape designer Edwin Lutyens, the gardens are a tribute to the thousands of Irish soldiers who died in World War I while serving in the British Army. The sombre design incorporates the War Stone and four granite pavilions, one of which contains Celtic and art deco illuminated manuscripts by the book illustrator Harry Clarke, listing the names of those killed in action.

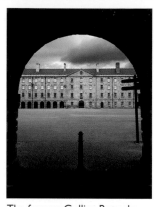

The former Collins Barracks – now a museum

On the north bank of the Liffey, behind Wolfe Tone Quay, are the former **Collins Barracks**. Built in 1701, the barracks were occupied continuously until 1997. Since then, they have been home to the **National Museum of Decorative Arts and History** (open Tues–Sat 10am–5pm, Sun 2–5pm; <www.museum.ie>). Silver, ceramics, furniture and folk artefacts trace Ireland's social and political history. There is also a café and bookshop.

The Liberties

Back towards the city centre now, and to the south of High Street, the area known as the **Liberties** was so named because it was situated outside the medieval city walls and was run by local courts, free of city regulations on trade. The area, once a slum, is rapidly gentrifying, with new housing and restoration of the original small red-brick houses.

Across from the two St Audoen's *(see page 44)*, two interesting streets run off High Street. Francis Street is lined with antiques shops, full of glittering treasures, and in Back Lane are the headquarters of An Taisce, an organisation dedicated to the preservation of historic buildings and gardens in Ireland. Its home is the delightful **Tailors' Hall**, the oldest guildhall in Ireland, once used by hosier and barber-surgeons' guilds as well as by the tailors. It dates from 1706, and is one of the few remaining original Queen Anne buildings in Dublin.

St Patrick's Cathedral

At the eastern end of Back Lane and turning right, Nicholas Street becomes Patrick Street. On the left, off St Patrick's Close, is **St Patrick's Cathedral** (open Mon–Sat 9am–6pm, Nov–Feb Sat until 5pm, times vary on Sundays; admission charge). This is the oldest Christian site in Dublin – St Patrick himself is reputed to have baptised converts on this spot (marked by a Celtic cross in the nave), suggesting that there has been a church here since around AD450. In the adjoining St Patrick's Park a marker shows the site of **St Patrick's Well**.

The height and space of the cathedral are impressive. Note the carved helmets and swords set above the choir stalls and the 19th-century tiled floor, similar to the one in Christ Church. The 90-m (300-ft) interior makes it the longest church in the country. The 45-m (150 ft) tower holds the largest ringing peal of bells in Ireland. Not much is left of the original construction

St Patrick's Cathedral choir

The grave of Jonathan Swift

of 1191. Destroyed in a fire in the 14th century, it was later rebuilt, and even includes some Victorian restoration work, though not as extensive as that in Christ Church.

The cathedral has had a varied history. From 1320, until it was closed by Henry VIII, St Patrick's was the seat of Ireland's first university. Later, Cromwellian troops used the aisles to stable their horses. The great Jonathan Swift, author of *Gulliver's Travels*, was dean here from 1713 to 1745. He was much revered for his charity and his championship of the Irish cause. You can see his grave and that of his great love, Esther Johnson, as well as the pulpit from which he preached. On the wall is his epitaph, written by himself.

An interesting artefact from the medieval chapter house is a door with a hole in it. The hole was cut in 1492 by Lord Kildare so he could reassure his arch enemy Lord Ormonde, who was under siege in the chapter house, of his friendly intentions. Kildare put his arm through the hole, thus giving rise to the common expression 'to chance your arm'.

Also in St Patrick's Close (left from the cathedral exit) is **Marsh's Library** (open Mon and Wed–Fri 10am–1pm and 2–5pm, Sat 10.30am–1pm; admission charge), the first public library in Ireland, founded in 1701 and holding more than 25,000 books, most dating from the 16th to the 18th century. The oak shelving is original, as are the metal cages in which scholars were locked so as to prevent thefts. Even if you aren't a scholar, do come here – the atmosphere and beauty of the place is entrancing.

GEORGIAN DUBLIN

Georgian architecture is found all over the city; however, the harmonious streets and squares lying to the southeast of Nassau Street truly deserve the title. In addition to uperb buildings, there are several important museums and galleries to visit, and the banks of the Grand Canal provide leafy, shaded walks.

Merrion Square

Clare Street, at the eastern end of Nassau Street, runs into **Merrion Square North**, where you'll find some of the finest houses. The square dates from 1762; houses here were the homes of high society, including many members of parliament and famous artists and writers. Look for individual details on the houses – the painted doors, the fanlights, and the door knockers, some in the form of a fish or a human hand.

Typical Georgian doorways on Merrion Square

On Merrion Square West is the National Gallery of Ireland, which provides tickets for free 40-minute tours of the restored **Government Buildings** (tours Sat from 10.30am–1.30pm on the hour, tickets available on the morning of the tour from the National Gallery; admission free) in Upper Merrion Street. Refurbished in 1990–91 and housing the offices and meeting rooms of the *Taoiseach* (Prime Minister) and his cabinet, the interior rooms of the buildings are a fascinating and tasteful combination of the old and the new. A magnificent Evie Hone stained-glass window adorns the landing in the main entrance; it is beautifully complemented by the carpet and balustrade designed by Mary Fitzgerald. There is some excellent contemporary furniture and a miniature of Oisín Kelly's sculpture *The Children of Lir*. Outside, the courtyard is paved in limestone tram-setts from the streets of Old Dublin.

The Natural History Museum

Also in Merrion Street, next to the front garden of Leinster House, is the Victorian collection of the **Natural History Museum** (open Tues–Sat 10am–5pm, Sun 2–5pm; free; <www.museum.ie>). This museum, opened in 1857 (with a speech by Dr Livingstone no less), holds an extensive collection zoological exhibits. Two giant Irish Deer skeletons are one of the first things you see. The cabinets are stuffed with mammals, birds, fish, butterflies and insects – it's popularly known as the 'Dead Zoo.' A favourite with children, it gives a fascinating glimpse into the late-Victorian obsession with travelling and collecting.

The **National Gallery of Ireland** (Mon–Sat 9.30am–5.30pm, Thur until 8.30pm, Sun noon–5.30pm; <www.nationalgallery.ie> is also

Picture this...

The addition of the Millennium Wing *(above)* has made the National Gallery a truly modern institution, but this was not always the case. In the late 1980s, the museum was in such a state of disrepair, one art-lover was able to steal a small French oil painting and post it back to the gallery in protest at the lack of care taken with the artworks.

free and houses a fine collection of works from the 14th to the 20th century – from Goya, Brueghel, Titian, Velasquez, Rembrandt and Gainsborough, to Monet, Degas and Picasso. One of the gallery's most important paintings, discovered in the house of the Jesuit Brothers in 1993, is Caravaggio's long-lost masterpiece, *The Taking of Christ*. There is also a fine

Statue of Oscar Wilde

collection of Irish art, including a whole roomful of Jack Yeats's paintings. There are also watercolours, drawings, prints, sculpture and a multimedia gallery offering information about 100 of the gallery's best works. With a good bookshop and the excellent Fitzer's café you could easily spend a day here. The Millennium Wing, a new extension to the museum, opened in 2002 and is used mostly for temporary exhibitions.

Enter one of the many gates of **Merrion Square Park** and walk along some of the secret, wooded paths to the immaculately groomed gardens. Don't miss Danny Osborne's **statue of Oscar Wilde**, wearing a smoking jacket with red lapels and reclining on a rock in the northeast corner of the park. At the height of the Great Famine in 1845–7, a soup kitchen was set up here to feed the starving. You'll want to return here to browse the **Boulevard Galleries** of art set up around the square on summer weekends.

Fitzwilliam Square and Beyond

Take time to stroll down the streets around Merrion Square, which were laid out at the same time as the square. At the eastern end of Upper Mount Street you'll notice the distinctive shape of the Greek-revival **St Stephen's Church**, which dates back to 1824. For obvious reasons it is known universally as the 'Pepper Canister Church'; occasional events and concerts are held here.

Lower Fitzwilliam Street, at the southeast corner of Merrion Square, houses the offices of the Electricity Supply Board. They tried to make up for the ugliness of their new premises by restoring **Number Twenty Nine** (open Tues–Sat 10am–5pm, Sun 1–5pm; admission charge) as a museum representing a typical bourgeois house of the period. And indeed, this lovely Georgian townhouse has been superbly fitted out to reflect middle-class life in the late 18th to early 19th century. An audio-visual display, cosily narrated by the 'ghost' of the former owner and her much put-upon maidservant, is followed by a half-hour guided tour for a maximum of ten people. The staff are friendly and helpful, and there is a small tearoom. The place can get very busy, though.

The street crosses Lower Baggot Street and leads on to **Fitzwilliam Square**, which has a park open to residents only. The last of Dublin's Georgian squares to be built, it was com-

Crossing Fitzwilliam Square in style

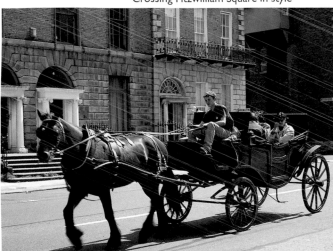

Patrick Kavanagh

Patrick Kavanagh was born in 1904 at Mucker, Inniskeen, County Monaghan. His father eeked a living from the land and by repairing the shoes that walked upon it. Young Patrick joined in these trades with little success. Local farmers made a joke of his farming skills and called him a fool for pursuing poetry. He moved to Dublin and in 1936 *Tarry Flynn*, his first publication, set his reputation on its way.

pleted by 1830, although the older houses date back to 1714. Here, as elsewhere in Georgian Dublin, there is exquisite detail in the doorways and fanlights, and the ironwork of the balconies.

Back in Baggot Street is the main office of the Bank of Ireland. The road was named after Baggotrath Castle, which stood here until the early 19th century. At Baggot Street Bridge you will find the headquarters of Bord Fáilte (the Irish Tourist Board).

If you turn right along the towpath of the **Grand Canal**, you can see a bronze statue of the Irish poet Patrick Kavanagh, who died in 1967; the poet is shown in relaxed pose, on a bench. The Grand Canal was begun in 1755. The pleasant towpath walk, under a canopy of leaves, goes past the gardens of terraced houses, offices and apartment buildings. There are plenty of ducks, moorhens and swans, and the canal is spanned by the distinctive curves of the 18th-century bridges. If you want more information about the canals, you can visit the **Waterways Visitor Centre** (closed for refurbishment, enquiries tel: 071 965 0787), on Grand Canal Quay. Opposite the centre and set in a restored sugar mill is the **Tower Design Centre**, comprising craft shops, workshops, and a first-floor restaurant.

Beyond Baggot Street Bridge to the east is the suburb of **Ballsbridge**, at the heart of which are the grounds of the **Royal Dublin Society** (RDS) where the famous Dublin (Kerry gold) Horse Show takes place.

NORTH OF THE RIVER

Dublin north of the Liffey has its own atmosphere and, like the southern part of the city, some magnificent buildings, museums, and Dublin's two most important theatres.

Along the Quays

Crossing **O'Connell Bridge**, there are fine views along the river. The Custom House is on the right and to the left is the equally splendid Four Courts. The bridge was built in 1790 and widened until it was almost square in 1880.

Turning left along the quays of the north bank towards the Four Courts (about 1.5km/1 mile), you will reach the cast-iron **Ha'penny Bridge**, which connects Merchants' Arch to Liffey Street. The footbridge was built in 1816, and its name refers to the toll once levied for crossing. Looking up river, the next bridge is the pedestrian **Millennium Bridge**. On the corner of Liffey Street is a **sculpture** known locally as 'the hags with the bags'. Two doors down from the bridge is the charming Winding Stair bookshop and restaurant.

The **Four Courts** was designed by James Gandon in 1785. With its Corinthian portico crowned with statues and its columned dome, the

Ha'penny Bridge

The imposing Four Courts

building is a majestic sight. It holds the various courts of the city, together with a law library and a restaurant. The building was damaged in the fighting of the 1920s and a fire destroyed all the official archives, but thorough restoration work was carried out in 1932. You can step inside when the courts are in session (open Mon–Fri 9.30am–4pm).

Turn north into Church Street to find **St Michan's Church** (open Mar–Oct, Mon–Fri 10am–12.45pm and 2pm–4.45pm; Nov–Mar, Mon–Fri 12.30–3.30pm; Sat all year 10am–12.45pm; admission charge for tours). Built in the 17th century on the site of a Danish chapel, the church's chief claim to fame is its vaults, which, because of their limestone composition, preserve bodies buried there in a mummified state. A few of the bodies are on display. Robert Emmet is thought to be buried in the graveyard of the church, and Parnell's funeral service was held here. Handel is said to have practised on the 1724 organ while composing *The Messiah*.

The **Old Jameson Distillery** (open daily 9.30am–6pm, last tour 5.30pm; admission charge) is in Smithfield, the heart of Old Dublin. If you ever wanted to know more about the fascinating craft of whiskey making, this award-winning attraction is the place to find out. Located on the original site of the Jameson Distillery in cobbled Bow Street, it also offers a history of the distillery itself. Behind the building, in Smithfield Market, is the **Chimney Viewing Tower** (open Mon–Sat 10am–5pm, Sun 11am–5pm; admission charge). The 56-m (185-ft) chimney from the old distillery is topped with a glass-enclosed platform, providing a panoramic view of the city.

If you turn right instead of left from O'Connell Bridge, you will come to one of Dublin's great architectural masterpieces, the **Custom House** (open mid-Mar–Nov Mon–Fri 10am–12.30pm, Sat–Sun 2–5pm; winter Wed–Fri and Sun only). Designed by James Gandon as his first Dublin masterpiece, it was built in 1791. The sculpture on the dome (a personification of Commerce) and the river gods (including Anna Livia, set over the main door) are by Edward Smyth, who was also responsible for the statues on the GPO *(see page 61)*. The north side of the building has statues by Joseph Banks depicting Africa, America, Asia and Europe.

On Custom House Quay is Dublin's **Famine Memorial**. Unveiled in 1998, this is a series of striking life-size bronze figures by sculptor Rowan Gillespie. Their gaunt and emaciated features are given added poignancy by the fact that they appear to be walking past the gleaming facade of the Allied Irish Bank, looking east towards the Irish Sea.

Famine Memorial

O'Connell Street

O'Connell Street is a grand boulevard with a wide central section, studded with monuments and statues. It runs in a straight line north from O'Connell Bridge, and the best way to view it is to walk down the central island, making excursions to the left and right at the zebra crossings.

The road was largely destroyed in the Rising *(see page 18)*, but was restored by the end of the 1920s. At the foot of the bridge is John Foley's **monument to Daniel O'Connell**, surrounded by four victory figures and peppered with bullet holes from 1922. The memorial to working-class hero, orator, and socialist **Jim Larkin** by Oisín Kelly is opposite the famous chiming clock of **Clerys**, one of the world's first purpose-built department stores founded in 1853. Farther up on the right is one of Dublin's legendary hotels, the Gresham, which was built in 1817, seven years before the Shelbourne.

Detail of the monument to Daniel O'Connell

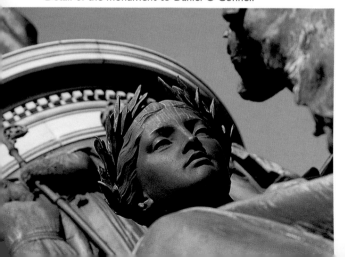

In the centre of O'Connell Street is the **General Post Office** (open Mon–Sat 8am–8pm, Sun 10am–6.30pm). Built in 1815–18, it is one of the last great buildings to come out of Dublin's Georgian boom, and is renowned for its imposing Ionic portico (look for the bullet holes) with six fluted columns and figures sculpted by Edward Smyth. It was here, in 1916, that James Connolly and Padraig Pearse barricaded themselves inside and proclaimed the Irish Republic. The post office was virtually destroyed in the fighting but has since been restored. The Rising is commemorated in the main hall by a beautiful bronze statue of the mythic folk hero **Cúchulainn** and by ten paintings illustrating various scenes of the rebellion.

Joyce statue

At the junction of O'Connell Street and North Earl Street is a statue of James Joyce, walking with a cane in his hand. It is known to the Dublin populace as the Prick with the Stick.

O'Connell Street Street has recently benefited from a rejuvenation programme that created a pedestrian plaza with trees, street furniture and special lighting in front of the GPO. Its newest monument, the **Spire of Dublin**, was erected in 2003 on the old site of Nelson's Pillar. It stands 120m (394ft) high and a time capsule has been sealed beneath it. Always quick with a witty moniker, Dubliners have taken to calling it the 'stiletto in the ghetto' or the 'stiffey by the Liffey'.

Just off Lower O'Connell Street on the corner of Lower Abbey and Marlborough streets is the **Abbey Theatre** (see page 89; <www.abbeytheatre.ie>). Founded in 1904 by W.B. Yeats, Lady Augusta Gregory and Edward Martyn, the theatre has long been a showcase for great Irish writing. The early works of Sean O'Casey and John Synge were written for the Abbey. The present theatre dates from 1966, since a fire in 1951 destroyed the original. It now forms part of the National Theatre, along with the Peacock Theatre just around the corner.

Situated just north of the Abbey Theatre in Marlborough Street is **St Mary's Pro-Cathedral** (open Mon–Fri 7.30am–6.45pm, Sat 7.30am–7.15pm, Sun 9am–1.45pm and 5.30–7.45pm; <www.procathedral.ie>) the main Catholic parish church of the city centre, built between 1816 and 1825. Its somewhat forbidding classical Doric exterior seems to dwarf the street (it was designed originally for O'Connell Street). The domed Renaissance interior is very plain, but the Palestrina choir that sings Mass here on Sundays is anything but, and attracts large numbers of visitors.

Opposite the cathedral is **Tyrone House** (not open to the public), home to the Department of Education. Built in 1742 by Richard Castle, the interior features work by the Francini brothers (also responsible for Newman House). Outside is a gift to the people of Ireland from the Italian government in gratitude for relief supplies during World War II: a marble Pietà entitled *La Deposizione*, by Ermenegildo Luppi.

Moore Street Market

It is worth making a detour on the pedestrianised areas of **Henry Street** and **Moore Street**, to see their famous markets and hear the cries of the stallholders *(see page 84)*. Expect some ribald remarks in broad Dublin accents. Moore Street Market is open Monday to Saturday and specialises in fruit, vegetable and flowers. This area is quickly becoming the multi-ethnic hub of Dublin's growing immigrant community. Alongside the fruit stalls are shops selling Russian, African and Chinese specialities.

At the northern end of the street is the 1911 **monument to Parnell** by Augustus St-Gaudens. Notice anything odd? Yes, he is wearing two overcoats (apparently he always did).

The man with two overcoats:
Charles Stewart Parnell

Parnell Square

Compared to the Georgian squares south of the Liffey, the area around **Parnell Square** looks rather shabby, but once it was just as fashionable and affluent. On the south side of Parnell Square are the **Rotunda Hospital** and the Gate Theatre. The Palladian-style Rotunda was built by Richard Castle in 1751–1755; it's Europe's oldest maternity hospital. The chapel on the first floor, with stained-glass windows and rococo plasterwork, has served at different times as an Assembly Room and a cinema; Charles Dickens also gave readings here. What is now the **Gate Theatre** *(see page 89;* <www.gate-theatre.ie>) was built in 1784 and is probably the most beautiful stage in Dublin. The theatre company was founded in 1930 by Michael MacLiammóir and Hilton Edwards, and is still going strong today, with an excellent reputation for international and innovative work. James Mason and Orson Welles began their acting careers here. The theatre is now a popular venue for contemporary music concerts.

The **Garden of Remembrance** on the north side of Parnell Square is dedicated to those who lost their lives in the cause of Irish freedom and features a cruciform lake and Oisín Kelly's beautiful sculpture of the *Children of Lir*.

Across the road from the garden, the **Dublin City Gallery, The Hugh Lane** (open Tues–Thur 10am–6pm, Fri–Sat 10am–5pm, Sun 11am–5pm, closed Mon; free; <www.hughlane.ie>) occupies a home built for Lord Charlemont by Sir William Chambers. Restored in 1991, this handsome building is worth seeing for itself alone, as well as for the splendid art collection. Sir Hugh Lane, who died in 1915, bequeathed his collection of paintings to the Irish government and the National Gallery in London. The collection includes works by Manet, Degas and other French impressionists as well as their Irish counterparts. The post-impressionist paintings of Jack B. Yeats (brother of the famous poet) are particularly noteworthy. The gallery has also acquired the Studio of Francis Bacon

James Joyce's Dublin

The Irish Catholic novelist, poet and short story-writer James Joyce (1882–1941) is best known for his controversial novel *Ulysses* (1922), which describes in minute detail a day in the life of advertising salesman Leopold Bloom as he makes his way through the city. Dublin had also played a part in two of Joyce's previous works, the short story collection *Dubliners* (1914), and the semi-autobiographical novel *A Portrait of the Artist as a Young Man* (1914–15). Joyce's descriptions of Dublin life in *Dubliners* are as evocative as they are gloomy – his city is one of 'dark muddy lanes' and 'dark dripping gardens'. Stephen Dedalus, the dissolute protagonist of *A Portrait of the Artist*, views Dublin in similarly despairing tones. This contrasts with Joyce's buoyant characterisation of Dublin in *Ulysses* as a vibrant, intellectually stimulating city. However the novel's linguistic complexities and general absence of plot will discourage all but the most determined readers.

and all its contents, which has been reconstructed here as a permanent exhibit (admission charge).

The **Dublin Writers Museum** next door (open Mon–Sat 10am–5pm, Sun 11am–5pm; Mon–Fri 10am–6pm June–Aug; admission charge; <www.writersmuseum.com>) is an intriguing combination of Georgian exterior and Victorian interior, also restored

The Dublin Writers Museum

in 1991. No one interested in Irish writing and theatre should miss this light and elegant museum covering the long Irish literary tradition, displaying first editions, theatre programmes, correspondence, clothing and other memorabilia. The collection begins with medieval Irish writing and ends with Brendan Behan, Liam O'Flaherty and Sean O'Faoláin. There are frequent exhibitions and events, and the Writers Centre provides a place for talk and work. Upstairs is a portrait gallery. There is a children's room and a bookshop, and a good café and restaurant.

East of Parnell Square, along North Great George's Street, is the **James Joyce Centre** (open Tues–Sat 10am–5pm; admission charge; <www.jamesjoyce.ie>). This interesting museum and cultural centre is housed in a mansion dating from 1784 and run by Joyce's nephew. The centre contains a library, exhibition rooms, and a study centre devoted to the great novelist. There is a full programme of events, including lectures, tours of the house and a walking tour of Joycean Dublin. Joyce himself must have known the house as the residence of Mr Denis J. Maginni, 'professor of dancing', who appears several times in the novel *Ulysses*.

Phoenix Park

On the banks of the Liffey, just 3km (2 miles) from the bustle of O'Connell Street, lies the biggest urban park in Europe, comprising some 709 hectares (1,750 acres) of landscaped gardens, woods, pastures and playing fields. The park is a graceful and elegant expanse with fine views of the mountains, much loved by Dubliners since it was first opened to the public in 1747. Self-guided heritage walks and nature trails are marked by black plaques.

The oldest building in the park is **Ashtown Castle**, a former papal residence which has been renovated to house the splendid **Phoenix Park Visitor Centre** (open Apr–Sept daily 10am–6pm, mid–end Mar and Oct daily 10am–5.30pm, Nov–mid-Mar Wed–Sun 10am–5pm; admission charge; wheelchair access), which presents a video and an excellent two-floor exhibition on the history and wildlife of the park. The castle itself comprises an early 17th-century tower house, restored with Irish oak from the park which is held together without a single nail. Outside there is a young garden maze, marking the outline of the original foundations, and a restful café.

The park also boasts the tallest obelisk in Europe in the 67-m (220-ft) **Wellington Monument**, erected in 1861 after the victory of Waterloo. The Wicklow granite is faced with plaques cast from captured and melted-down cannon. Not quite as large is the **Papal Cross**, commemorating Pope John Paul II's visit in 1979, when more than one million people gathered to celebrate Mass.

The **Phoenix Column**, dating from 1747, stands near the natural spring from which the name of the park is derived (the result of an English corruption of the Gaelic *fionn uisce*, meaning 'clear water').

Occupying more than 26 hectares (66 acres), the **Dublin Zoo** (open Mon–Sat from 9am, Sunday from 10.30am; closing times vary from 3.30pm in Oct to 6.30pm from

Apr–Sept; admission charge; <www.dublinzoo.ie>;) was founded in 1831. The landscaped grounds (designed by Decimus Burton, who was also responsible for the park lodges) provide a safe home to more than 700 species, including such endangered animals as snow leopards and golden lion tamarinds. A highlight is the African Plains, which provides a spacious home for its large species. The Nakuru Safari tour takes visitors through the area.

The Wellington Monument

Also within the sprawling grounds of the park are the official residence of the Irish president, which dates from 1751 (guided tours from the visitor centre Sat 10.15am–4.30pm, until 3.30pm in winter; <www.president.ie>), and the US ambassador's residence, an 18th-century house which was formerly the official residence of the Viceroy's chief secretary (not open to the public).

Just to the north-west of Phoenix Park is **Farmleigh House** (open Mar–Dec Thur–Sun 10.30am–5pm; <www.farmleigh. ie>). This grand estate of 78 acres was bought by the government from the Guinness family and has been carefully refurbished. Today it's used as accommodation for visiting dignitaries, for high-level meetings and for the public enjoyment. The interior is beautifully presented and the Victorian Courtyard hosts food markets in the spring and summer.

EXCURSIONS

South of the City

As if the city itself did not provide enough options, the countryside around Dublin offers a wealth of possible excursions and day trips. The DART railway, running north and south to nearby seaside towns and villages, offers a scenic trip along the coast. If you take the DART south, you'll find the best sandy beaches in Dublin.

Dún Laoghaire is the major port on the east coast. Here, ferries across the Irish Sea leave from two state-of-the-art piers. West of the harbour is the ramshackle National Maritime Museum. The penultimate stop on the DART is **Bray**, a faded seaside resort with a beach and amusement arcades. There are splendid views from Bray Head of the harbour and the mountains. You can take the DART on to its terminus at **Greystones**, a pretty coastal town, or you can walk there along the coast from Bray, though parts of the path are in poor condition.

County Wicklow, also to the south of Dublin, rightly deserves its title, 'Garden of Ireland', with some of the most spectacular scenery in the country: rugged mountains, steep,

Getting Out

Many bus tours will take you to the various destinations (see page 115), and some are accessible by city bus. Dublin Tourism at Suffolk Street has all the information, and can arrange tours. Car hire is available at the same site (see page 108). It is worthwhile to hire a car so you can go at your own pace. The suggestions for excursions in this section can all be done in a day or a half day from the city; most entries indicate how the destination can be reached. Note that some attractions can be seen only by guided tour, and the last admission to these may be 30 to 45 minutes earlier than the official closing time.

wooded river valleys, and deep lakes as well as charming villages and some notable mansions and gardens.

James Joyce Museum

Interior of the Joyce Museum

At Sandycove in County Dublin the **James Joyce Museum** (open Mar–Oct Mon–Sat 10am–1pm and 2–5pm, Sun 2–6pm; Nov–Feb by appointment only, tel: 280 9265; admission charge) is one of the most unusual small museums in or around Dublin. It is housed in a Martello Tower. A series of such towers, some 12m (40ft) high and 2.5m (8ft) thick, were constructed along the coast at the beginning of the 19th century to guard against invasion by Napoleon. Joyce actually lived in the tower very briefly, and it is the location for the first chapter of *Ulysses*. Full of Joycean memorabilia (including his guitar and waistcoat), correspondence, and rare editions of books and manuscripts, it is a shrine for Joyce enthusiasts. DART to Glasthule.

Avoca

The picturesque village of **Avoca** in County Wicklow became famous as the setting for the BBC TV series *Ballykissangel*. A company of handweavers has been working here since at least 1723, and visitors are able to watch them as they work; unfortunately, though, their products are somewhat less distinctive since the place became a popular tourist attraction. There's a colourful shop and a popular café in the small complex of traditional buildings (open summer daily 9am–6pm; winter 9.30am–5.30pm).

St Kevin

St Kevin, founder of the monastery at Glendalough, was famed for his patience. One story tells how a bird laid an egg in the palm of his hand; to avoid causing harm, the holy man stayed still until the egg hatched.

Glendalough

Set in a beautiful landscape, with clear lakes and streams surrounded by steep wooded hills, the sacred site of **Glendalough** (from the Irish for 'Valley of the Two Lakes', or Gleann Dá Locha) in the Wicklow Mountains, is still highly evocative, and should not be missed. It was the place chosen by St Kevin for a monastery which, over the centuries, became a great spiritual centre of learning, attracting pilgrims from all over Europe. Despite Viking raids, a great fire at the end of the 14th century and long years of neglect, many of the original buildings still stand at Glendalough: the 11th-century round tower (30m/ 100ft high and 15m/50ft around the base), a 9th-century barrel-vaulted church known as 'St Kevin's Kitchen' and the roofless cathedral. There are also scores of Celtic crosses.

The site can be visited by car or bus tour, or by taking St Kevin's bus from the north side of St Stephen's Green near Grafton Street (leave 11.30am, arrive 1pm, return 4.30pm; <www.glendaloughbus.com>). The visitor centre (open mid-Mar–mid-Oct 9.30am–6pm, until 5pm in winter) provides a 20-minute audiovisual presentation of the history of Irish monasticism, plus an exhibition on the geology and wildlife of the area, and conducts guided tours – but you can also wander about on your own. Glendalough's three nature trails take under an hour's relaxed walking and are well worth doing.

Glendalough is part of the **Wicklow Mountains National Park**, an area of about 200 sq km (78 sq miles), which includes most of upland Wicklow, with spectacular scenery, wildlife and rare flora. The 137-km (85-mile) **Wicklow Way** long-distance footpath wends its course through the park.

Mount Usher Gardens

The spectacular **Mount Usher Gardens** (open Apr–Oct daily 10.30am–6pm; admission charge; car or bus tours) were established in 1868 by the Walpole family. The climate and soil are such that plants and trees that would not normally survive this far north are capable of flourishing, which explains the enormous variety of more than 4,000 plants, trees and shrubs from all over the world. The 8-hectare (20-acre) paradise is near Ashford, along the River Vartry. It attracts a range of birds and wildfowl. There is a tearoom on site.

Powerscourt

About 18km (12 miles) from Dublin, outside the pretty village of Enniskerry in the foothills of the Wicklow Mountains, is the **Powerscourt House and Gardens** (open daily, 9.30am–5.30pm; gardens close at dusk in winter; guided

Glendalough is a big draw for tourists

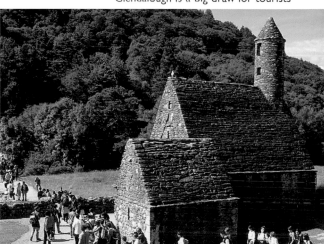

tours available; admission charge). It consists of some 5,500 hectares (14,000 acres), hugging the River Dargle. The gardens are among the greatest in Europe, and take in a view of the Sugar Loaf Mountain as part of their design. The enormous Palladian house regrettably was destroyed by fire in 1974. The house now incorporates the restored ballroom, a restaurant overlooking the gardens, an exhibition on the history of the estate, several shops and a garden centre.

The formal splendour of the grounds testifies to the 18th-century desire to tame nature, but it is done with such superlative results that one can only be thankful that the work was undertaken. The sweeping terraces offer magnificent views; statuary rears up out of ornamental lakes; deer roam the parklands; and the Dargle obligingly throws itself over 122m (400ft) of rock to form the highest waterfall in Ireland (4km/2½ miles from the main estate). Children like the pets' cemetery.

The grandiose Powerscourt Estate

Russborough House

This magnificent Georgian-Palladian house at Blessington (open for guided tours only, May–Sept daily 10am–5pm; Apr and Oct Sun and holidays 10am–5pm; admission charge), constructed in 1740–1750 and designed by Richard Castle, is one of the earliest Irish great houses. It is constructed on a monumental scale, with a 213-m (700-ft) facade of Wicklow granite, Doric arcades and wonderful ornamentation, all set against an impressive terraced landscape, with the extensive grounds covering some 80 hectares (200 acres).

Irish country houses are generally distinguished by their architecture rather than their contents, but Russborough is a striking exception to this rule. The interiors feature superb plasterwork by the Francini brothers, identifiable, as elsewhere, by their trademark of eagles' heads. The plasterwork on the staircase, with its lavish swags of flowers gently held in the mouths of some very patient-looking dogs is extraordinary. The inlaid floors are particularly lovely, and there are extensive collections of furniture, silver and tapestries.

Also in the house is the impressive **Beit Collection** of paintings, which is shared with the National Gallery; it includes celebrated works by Gainsborough, Goya, Guardi, Hals, Reynolds, Rubens, Velasquez, Vermeer and others, and a series of eight paintings by Murillo depicting the story of the prodigal son.

West of the City

When William Connolly, then speaker of the Irish House of Commons, set his heart on a palatial country home, he turned to Italian architect Alessandro Galilei, who designed the facade of **Castletown House**, at Celbridge, County Kildare, in 1722. This Palladian masterpiece, however, was finished by Irishman Edward Lovett Pearce who is responsible for the colonnades and side pavilions. The result is one of the most graceful and distinctive houses of the period in Ireland. The house's famous Long Gallery has Pompeiian fresco-inspired designs and Venetian chandeliers; the great staircase is the work of Simon Vierpyl; and the plasterwork is by the Francinis. The grounds (now sadly encroached upon) are adorned by a 48-m (140-ft) high obelisk. (Open mid-Apr–Sept Mon–Fri 10am–6pm, Sat– Sun 1–6pm; Oct Mon–Fri 10am–5pm, Sun 1–5pm; Nov Sun 1–5pm; admission charge; car or bus 67/67A followed by a half-mile walk.)

Irish National Stud and Japanese Gardens

Horses are immensely popular in Ireland, and County Kildare can claim to be at the heart of horse country. The Curragh and Punchestown racecourses are situated here, and the **Irish National Stud** at Tully (open mid-Feb–mid-Nov daily 9.30am–5pm; admission charge; combined ticket covers Irish Stud, Irish Horse Museum, Japanese Gardens and St Fiachras Garden), home to breeding stallions, has produced some of the most successful horses in the country. Visitors see horses being trained and exercised. There is also a museum illustrating the history of the horse in Ireland, which features the skeleton of the racehorse Arkle.

Adjacent to the stud are the **Japanese Gardens**, created by the stud's founder in the early part of the century, and well worth a visit, and the new **St Fiachras Garden**, created to celebrate the millennium.

North of the City

To the north of Dublin, the DART will take you to the **Howth** peninsula, which affords splendid views along a cliff-top coastal walk. In spring and summer this area is suffused with nesting sea birds, as well as interesting land birds and butterflies attracted by the moorland terrain of the cliff top. In July and August there is a wonderful colour combination of

The trawler dock at Howth

purple heather and yellow gorse. When walking up to the lighthouse, it is difficult to believe that Dublin is just a few miles away – until you see Dublin Bay spread out before you. Also located in Howth is the **National Transport Museum** (open June–Aug Mon–Sat 10am–5pm; Sept–May Sat–Sun 2–5pm) at Howth Castle.

National Botanic Gardens

Originally modelled on London's Kew Gardens, Ireland's pre-mier horticultural attraction, the **National Botanic Gardens** at Glasnevin (open end Oct–Feb daily 9am–4.30pm, beg of Feb to end Oct daily 9am–6pm; glasshouse closes 5pm Mon–Fr, 5.45pm Sat and Sun; free), was established by the Royal Dublin Society in 1795. With over 20,000 species in more than 20 hectares (50 acres) of grounds, there is plenty to see and enjoy in any season. Built between 1843 and 1868, the four magnificently restored glasshouse groups include an

Brendan Behan's grave at Glasnevin Cemetery

alpine house, a palm and orchid house, and the Curvilinear Range, a spectacular curving glass-house of cast iron. There are all sorts of different gardens and landscapes, including a pleasant riverside walk.

Adjacent to the gardens is the **Glasnevin Cemetery**, where some of the most notable figures in recent Irish history are buried. These include Charles Stewart Parnell, Daniel O'Connell and Éamon de Valera.

Casino Marino

Located on the Malahide Road 3 miles (5km) from the centre of Dublin, Lord Charlemont's 'small house by the sea', built in 1762– 77, is regarded as the finest neoclassical building in Ireland. The masterpiece of William Chambers, it is a work of great ingenuity: from the outside it looks like a small Greek-style temple, but is in fact two storeys high and contains eight rooms; to preserve the harmonious design the four corner columns are hollow to carry water off the roof, and the urns on roof are disguised chimneys. The interior has exquisite floors and plasterwork (open May and Oct daily 10am–5pm; June–Sept daily 10am–6pm; Apr Sat–Sun noon–5pm; Nov–Mar Sat–Sun noon–4pm; admission charge).

The Casino still stands in perfect splendour on a gentle rise. Down the road is 'Spite Crescent', built by an enemy of Lord Charlemont to spoil his view from the Casino. It was here that Bram Stoker stayed while writing *Dracula* in 1897.

Malahide Castle

The crenellated **Malahide Castle and Estate** (guided tours only Mon–Sat year-round 10am–5pm; Sun Apr–Sept 10am–6pm, Oct–Mar 11am–5pm; closed for tours 12.45–2pm; <www.malahidecastle.com>) in the pretty seaside town of Malahide (DART station) has been home to the Talbot family for 800 years, and parts of the building date back to the 12th century. The house is a showcase for some of the National Portrait Collection of the National Gallery and also contains fine 18th-century furniture, chinoiserie and children's toys. There are some impressive views of the grounds and distant mountains, particularly from the turret rooms. Audio tapes in each room narrate the house's history.

The lush park surrounding Malahide includes the **Talbot Botanic Gardens** (open May–Sept daily 2–5pm; admission charge), 8 hectares (20 acres) of walled gardens and glasshouses with thousands of plant species. Also in the grounds is the **Fry Model Railway Museum** (open Apr–Sept Mon–Thur and Sat 10am–5pm, Sun 2–6pm; closed for lunch 1–2pm Fri and Oct–Mar; admission charge), Ireland's largest O-gauge model railway, with miniature models of trains, railway stations and some of Dublin's landmarks.

Malahide Castle

Newbridge House and Victorian Farm

Newbridge House (open Apr–Sept Tues–Sat 10am–5pm, Sun 2–6pm, closed for lunch 1–2pm; Oct–Mar weekends only 12–5pm; admission charge) and its estate of some 142 hectares (350 acres) at Donabate, County Dublin, belonged to the Cobbe family from 1736. The beautifully restored house contains some interesting furniture and plasterwork, and there is also a museum of rural life incorporating several artisans' cottages with period furniture and tools.

Newgrange

Newgrange (open from dawn to dusk; admission charge) is the most important of the prehistoric sites around Dublin, located about 3km (2 miles) east of Slane in County Meath. It is the best preserved passage tomb in Europe, and is 500 years older than the Pyramids (3000BC). It's a huge mound (nearly 12m/40ft high and almost 90m/300ft wide) and is constructed from 200,000 tons of stone, much of which was somehow hauled from the Wicklow Mountains and the Mountains of Mourne. Newgrange may be the world's oldest solar observatory – the whole edifice is aligned in such a way that for several days of the winter solstice, light from the sun floods the inner chamber for around 17 minutes, a spectacular effect: the guide on the tour attempts to give an idea of this effect by plunging the chamber into darkness and slowly bringing up the light.

Nearby is **Knowth**, an even larger and older complex which dates back to earliest neolithic times. Knowth has two passage graves. The site is still being excavated, and only part of it is open. Guided tours for both sites originate from the nearby **Brú na Bóinne Centre** (open May and late-Sept daily 9am–6pm; June–mid-Sept 9am–7pm; Oct, Mar and Apr 9.30am–5.30pm; Nov–Feb 9.30am–5pm; admission charge), which has some interesting exhibits.

Tara

Tara, situated south of the busy town of Navan in County Meath, is a familiar name in Celtic myths and legends. The site was the cultural, political and religious centre of early Celtic civilisation and is reputedly where the high kings had their palace. Its importance waned, however, after the arrival of Christianity, and nowadays there's little to see except the hill, the remains of an Iron-Age fort, some pillar stones and the rewarding views over the central Irish plain. In a nearby 19th-century Anglican church is the **visitor centre** (open May–Oct daily 10am–6pm; admission charge), with exhibits and an audiovisual show. Guided tours are conducted of the site – they begin at the visitors' centre and lead past earthworks and ditches with evocative names such as *Rath na Riogh* (Wall of the Kings) and *Dumha Na nGiall* (Ditch of the Hostages).

The huge prehistoric mound at Newgrange

WHAT TO DO

Dublin is rapidly becoming a 24-hour city, so there is plenty to enjoy when your sightseeing is done. The city's many pubs are the centre of social life, offering conversation and a quiet pint, food, music and song. There are also lots of late-night clubs and bars. And with first-class shops and a profusion of booksellers, galleries and antiques dealers, you can browse or buy contentedly. If you're feeling active, there are excellent opportunities for sports.

PUBS

As you walk through Dublin's streets it will sometimes seem that there's a pub on every corner. Pubs are Ireland's living rooms – they provide not only drink and food, but atmosphere, entertainment and amusing talk. You may not fall into conversation in Dublin quite as readily as in a country pub, but you'll find that here, as everywhere, the Irish are welcoming hosts. Most pubs also serve food – they are good places to have lunch – and some have dining rooms. Be warned that the pubs around O'Connell Street can be rough, and at times Temple Bar pubs can be rowdy as they are favoured by visiting stag parties. Pubs open around 11am and close at 12.30am.

The oldest pub in Dublin is reputedly the Brazen Head (Bridge Street Lower) where, it is claimed, a tavern has stood since the 12th century. Wolfe Tone and his United Irishmen are believed to have

Time to settle

When you order a Guinness, the bartender fills the glass three quarters and lets it settle before topping it off. Do the same before you take a drink. It should be a smooth, dark black before you tip it back.

met here to plan their rebellion. It's cosy and intimate, with its cobblestone courtyard, and they serve a good pint of Guinness. Other authentic old Dublin pubs include Toner's (Lower Baggot Street), Mulligans (Poolbeg Street), Ryan's (Parkgate Street) and the Long Hall (South Great George's Street) with (reputedly) the city's longest bar counter.

Whatever you are looking for in a pub, Dublin will gladly provide. If you're after traditional music, O'Donoghue's (Merrion Row) and Slattery's (Capel Street) are still among Dublin's best; O'Donoghue's was formerly the haunt of The Dubliners. Jack Nealon's (also in Capel Street) has jazz on Sunday and eclectic music the rest of the week. Mother Redcap's Tavern (Back Lane, off High Street) is a big, relaxed place, also with live music. If you like traditional dancing, go to O'Shea's Merchant (Bridge Street Lower). The Stag's Head (Dame Court) is known for its good food and wonderful old wooden interior.

Irish pubs are the best place to meet and greet locals

Off Grafton Street is Kehoe's (South Anne Street), a favourite watering hole; and on Duke Street are two pubs with *Ulysses* connections – Davy Byrne's, where Leopold Bloom ate a gorgonzola sandwich and drank a glass of wine, and Bailey's, a busy, trendy and gay-friendly bar on the site of Leopold Bloom's house. Behind the Gaiety Theatre, you'll probably encounter a theatrical crowd in Neary's (Chatham Street). Microbreweries have also appeared in Dublin, and sell their excellent beers at the Dublin Brewing Company (North King Street) and Porterhouse Brewing Company (Parliament Street).

There are many old pubs in Temple Bar, but they are often twee and tourist choked. If you fancy a pint, then opt for some of the least offensive including the Oliver St John Gogarty (Fleet Street), named for the man-of-letters who was the model for a character in *Ulysees*, which has good traditional and other music. There's music upstairs in the small, quaint Ha'penny Bridge Inn (Wellington Quay). The Temple Bar (Temple Bar) attracts a busy, lively crowd; the Norseman (East Essex Street) is favoured by the art crowd, while the Auld Dubliner (Anglesea Street) is a pleasant pub that caters a lot for tourists. Make sure to drop in to the elegant old Palace on Fleet Street; with its beautiful interior and buzzy atmosphere it's popular with journalists from the nearby Irish Times.

If you're after a taste of modern Dublin, then there are chic, sleek pubs dotted throughout the city that present a good alternative to the traditional pubs. The Clarendon (Clarendon Street) is a glass-fronted spot with excellent food and good views from the top floor; The Market Bar (Fade Street) is an enormous bar that somehow oozes charm and atmosphere despite its gargantuan size; The South William on South William Street serves gastro pies with its pints; and the Shelbourne Bar is a hit among the Dublin's fickle fashion and media set.

Whether you drink alcohol or not, a trip to Dublin isn't complete without a visit to some of its pubs.

Shoppers on Grafton Street

SHOPPING

The main shopping areas are in and around Grafton Street, along Nassau Street, in Temple Bar, O'Connell Street, and Henry Street. Pedestrian Grafton Street is lined with well-known chains such as Marks and Spencer, the Body Shop, HMV records and Laura Ashley, plus the excellent, up-market Brown Thomas department store. O'Connell Street has more downmarket shops, but two landmarks are still here: Eason's for books and art supplies, and Clerys department store, with its famous chiming clock.

Shopping Centres

The three-storey **St Stephen's Green Shopping Centre** is at the top of Grafton Street overlooking the famous urban park. It boasts three floors of shops, but none really stand out and many are chains. It's worth a look if you need to pick up something in the large and good value Dunnes Stores with homewares, men's, women's and kids fashion and a supermarket. There's also a large Boots chemist and a branch of Hughes and Hughes bookstores. The **Powerscourt Townhouse** on Clarendon Street (follow the sign from Grafton Street) is more upmarket, and specialises in restaurants and cafés, and antiques, jewellery and designer clothing. Also on Clarendon Street is the smaller **Westbury Mall**, with cafés and fine jewellery shops. Further along, you'll find Drury Street and South William Street with some good quirky shops including Dublin's best vintage store Jenny Vander (Drury Street) the delectable Cherche Midi shoe shop (Drury Street), and Oakes, popular Irish designers with ready-to-wear and made-to-measure designs (South William Street). At Castle Market make sure to pop in for a browse around the elegant designer boutique Costume and the sophisticated Helen McAlinden store with soft furnishings and women's designs.

On the other side of Grafton Street, leading into Dawson Street, the **Royal Hibernian Way** is another small shopping mall with some exclusive shops. Dawson Street is lined with bookshops and boutiques. North of the river, the **Jervis Centre** on Henry Street has a selection of shops and department stores, including many UK chains. At the **ILAC Centre**, also on Henry Street, you'll find numerous clothes shops and a large branch of Dunnes Stores, an Irish clothes- and food-shop chain.

Markets

The oldest is on **Moore Street** (open Mon–Sat). It's famous for the cries of its sellers – the models for Molly Malone of the well-known song. Fruit, vegetables, electronics and a little bit of everything else is on sale here. It's also the place to go to pick up ethnic food and goods.

Moore Street Market

Pretty **George's Street Arcade** (open Mon–Sat) is a covered market between South Great George's and Drury streets. Shops and stalls line this atmospheric little market – a good place

George's Street Arcade

for secondhand books, art, music, vintage clothing and a variety of ethnic ware.

The **Temple Bar Food Market** (open Sat 10am–5.30pm) at Meeting House Square turns this touristy centre into the home of speciality foods and gourmet delights. It's also worth heading to the Old City section of Temple Bar where as well as a good range of chic interiors stores, you'll find the trendy Cow's Lane Fashion and Design Market (summer only; Sat only from 10am–5.30pm) with innovative designers and a hip vibe. Also on Saturday and Sunday, **Blackrock Market** (Sat 11am–5.30pm, Sun noon–5.30pm; on Main Street, near Blackrock DART station) has stalls selling jewellery, designer crafts, books, antiques and clothes.

What to Buy

Antiques. There are antiques fairs in Newman House on St Stephen's Green South every second Sunday all year. And don't miss a stroll down Francis Street, Dublin's 'antiques highway', lined with antiques and art stores. Also check out the lovely antiques shops on the second floor of Powerscourt Townhouse.

Art. For contemporary art, especially the work of Irish artists, you should try the Kerlin Gallery (off South Anne Street), the Taylor Galleries (Kildare Street), or the Solomon Gallery (Powerscourt Townhouse). The Temple Bar Gallery (Temple Bar) exhibits the work of up to 40 resident artists and the Apollo Art Gallery on Dawson Street has an equally impressive, if more dishevelled collection for sale.

Books. Eason's on O'Connell Street is a huge shop with mainstream books, magazines, newspapers and art supplies. Waterstone's and Hodges Figgis (of *Ulysses* fame) are across the street from each other in Dawson Street. Both carry an excellent selection of literature, general books, books on Ireland, and the works of Irish writers. International Books in South Frederick Street specialises in languages. For antiquarian books, go to Cathach Books in Duke Street. In Temple Bar, the bookshop at the Gallery of Photography carries a large selection of photographic publications. The labyrinthine Winding Stair on Ormond Quay is an interesting secondhand bookshop with a restaurant.

Chocolates. Delicious Irish handmade chocolates are on sale at Butler's Irish Chocolates in Grafton Street.

Crafts. The most distinguished place for modern Irish crafts is DESIGNyard in Nassau Street with its outstanding selection of jewellery, sculpture and contemporary design. The Irish Celtic Craftshop (Lord Edward Street) offers more traditional crafts. The Kilkenny Shop is a good hunting ground for everything from John Rocha-designed Waterford Crystal to Orla Kiely designer wellies, while you'll find a good range of traditional pottery of all shapes and sizes at Louis Mulcahy (Dawson Street).

Crystal. Ireland has long been known for its fine crystal, with famous brands including Waterford Crystal, Cavan,

Galway, Tipperary and Tyrone Crystal. Irish designers John Rocha and Louise Kennedy also do more contemporary lines for Waterford and Tipperary Crystal respectively. Prices do not vary. Try the House of Ireland, or the Tipperary Crystal on Eastmoreland Lane, Upper Baggot Street. The larger department stores are good places to find designer crystal lines.

Family Crests. There is a vast number of shops specialising in coats of arms on everything from plaques to keychains. Try Heraldic Artists and House of Names, both on Nassau Street.

Food. The Irish supermarket chain, Dunnes Stores (outlets on Middle Abbey Street, St Stephen's Green Shopping Centre, the ILAC Centre) sells Irish smoked salmon: ask for the wild, not farmed, variety. For Irish country cheeses, go to Sheridan Cheesemongers on South Anne Street.

Knitwear. There are two kinds of knits for sale: expensive traditional handknit sweaters and sweaters 'handknit' on a machine. For the former, go to the House of Ireland on Nassau Street. For the latter, bargains can be found at Blarney Woollen Mills (Nassau Street) and Dublin Woollen Mills (Lower Ormond Quay). The Kilkenny Shop on Nassau street carries a large variety of knitwear and handwoven goods. Monaghan's (Grafton Arcade) specialises in cashmere.

Linens. Brown Thomas has a great linen department. On the south end of Dawson Street is Needlecraft, specialising in fine Irish linens.

Music. For indigenous music, Celtic Note (Nassau Street) and Claddagh Records (Temple Bar) carry a good selection of traditional Irish and other Irish recordings. You can't miss HMV on Grafton Street. Road Records (Fade Street) and Selectah Records (Crow Street) specialise in dance and indie.

Photography. If you're looking for memory cards, batteries and printers any of the following should be of help: City Cameras on Dawson Street, One Hour Photo on St Stephens Green North, or the Camera Centre and Spectra Photo on

Grafton Street. For used as well as new equipment, try the Dublin Camera Exchange on Trinity Street.

Pottery and Porcelain. In Nassau Street the Kilkenny Shop has a fine selection. Louis Mulcahy on Dawson Street is also a wonderful treasure chest of handcrafted pottery.

Souvenirs. Shopping for souvenirs should be an easy task in Dublin. Nassau Street is the best destination for souvenir shops on the quick. Some shops may not be too original, but they have all the trinkets folks back home will be happy to get their hands on. If you have more time, there are some excellent shops spread throughout the city showcasing Irish crafts and design.

Wine. Vaughan Johnson's Fine Wine Shop, Mitchell and Sons on Kildare Street and Berry Bros & Rudd on Harry Street provide a tasty alternative to the world of Guinness and whiskey.

Inexpensive souvenirs of a stay in Dublin

The Gate Theatre

ENTERTAINMENT

Theatre

Dublin has a proud tradition in theatre which is still very much alive, so advance booking is advisable. The **Abbey Theatre** in Lower Abbey Street is Ireland's national theatre *(see also page 91)*. Once on the cutting edge, today its more experimental repertoire is presented on its second, basement stage, the intimate **Peacock**. The **Gate Theatre** in Parnell Square, has a similar tradition, and stages a cosmopolitan mix of Irish and international theatre plus musical acts. It's known for showcasing important new Irish playwrights.

The Victorian **Olympia** in Dame Street is the venue for all sorts of popular theatre, concerts and variety shows. The **Gaiety Theatre** in South King Street is worth visiting for its ornate décor alone. It runs a range of productions from plays to variety acts. For cutting edge theatre, the **Project Arts Centre** in East Essex Street has a lively programme of dance, drama, and performance arts, while **Andrew's Lane** also puts on modern productions. The **Samuel Beckett Theatre** at Trinity College is mainly for drama students.

Other theatres of note include the **Civic Theatre** outside the city in Tallaght, with its broad repertoire of music, drama and comedy productions; the **Point** theatre, a large venue that puts on limited runs of big, Broadway-type productions, comedy and high profile concerts. The **Lambert Puppet Theatre** in Monkstown is popular with children.

The most important event of the theatre season is the **Dublin Theatre Festival**, held in September–October each year. The festival is a showcase both for high quality international productions and for new Irish plays trying to break into the circuit. A fringe festival precedes this event annually.

Comedy

The International Bar on Wicklow Street has given the start to many Irish comedians and is still going strong. The revamped Laughter Lounge at Eden Quay is Ireland's premier comedy spot with gigs on Thursday, Friday and Saturday nights.

Ireland's National Theatre

Dublin's first theatre opened in 1637, and thereafter the city produced many notable playwrights, including Sheridan, Goldsmith, Wilde and Shaw, but there was nothing particularly 'Irish' about their work. W. B. Yeats wanted to create a distinctly Irish theatre of poetic drama, and he turned for inspiration to the legends of ancient Ireland. He looked for a backer, and found Lady Augusta Gregory, who became his partner. Their first productions were done on a shoestring, wherever they could find a space. Finally, in 1904, they acquired a theatre of their own, and the Abbey was born.

The Abbey's career was not without controversy. J. M. Synge's play, *The Playboy of the Western World*, now recognised as a masterpiece, provoked a riot when it was first staged. Later on, *The Plough and the Stars*, by the Abbey's first great realist playwright, Sean O'Casey, caused similar public outrage, and the police were called to protect the theatre.

After Yeats's death in 1939, the Abbey entered a period of limbo, although its acting tradition continued to be world renowned. Things turned around with the opening of its new theatre in 1966 and the emergence of new Irish playwrights – Brian Friel, Conor McPherson, and Frank McGuinness among others. Today, the Abbey continues its tradition of commitment to new work by Irish authors in both English and Gaelic.

Classical Music and Opera

The National Symphony Orchestra can be heard in a year-round programme of concerts at the **National Concert Hall** (NCH) in Earlsfort Terrace. The NCH also hosts jazz and traditional music evenings. Chamber music concerts and recitals are given at the **Irish Museum of Modern Art** at the beautiful Royal Hospital building in Kilmainham. **St Anne's Church** on Dawson Street has lunchtime concerts and the **Bank of Ireland Arts Centre** in Foster Place off College Green has lunchtime and evening concert series. Another venue for classical music is the huge **Helix** complex at the Dublin City University campus on Collins Avenue. Dublin also has a number of music festivals *(see* Calendar of Events *on page 97)*.

Opera Ireland offers short spring and winter seasons based on the standard repertoire at the **Gaiety Theatre** in King Street. The **Lyric** company have several productions a year, involving

Traditional Music

The word *seisiún* – meaning an impromptu evening of music and song, usually in a pub – has a particular resonance for the Irish, and there is plenty of opportunity in Dublin to enjoy traditional Irish sounds. A *seisiún* may start when someone – probably the innocent-looking man sitting in the corner huddled over a pint of Guinness – produces a guitar as if from nowhere, and his neighbour responds by bringing out a well-concealed *bodhrán* (goatskin traditional Irish drum). Soon everyone is joining in.

The mainstay of traditional music is the fiddle. The guitar is something of a latecomer, having arrived around the 1960s, but now it's well established. Other instruments you may hear are the uillean pipes (softer than the Scottish bagpipe), the six-hole wooden flute, the tin whistle, the accordion and the banjo, a transfer from America in the 19th century.

While the real centre of traditional music is in the west, you'll find it played in pubs across Dublin; watch for listings or signs in the pubs.

international artists at various venues. The small but enterprising Opera Theatre Company does two or three performances a year of short operas by contemporary Irish or baroque composers.

Irish flautist

Rock, Folk and Jazz

One of Dublin's largest venues is the Point, East Link Bridge, which hosts major pop and rock acts (the smash hit *Riverdance* was staged here). The RDS in Ballsbridge also occasionally holds huge open-air concerts. The *Irish Times* carries listings for all such events, and *In Dublin* has up-to-the-minute information. Some of the best music is heard at the mid-size venues: the **Olympia Theatre**, the **Ambassador** (O'Connell Street) and the **Temple Bar Music Centre** in Curved Street, where you can hear everything from local acts to international artists. **Whelans** on Wexford Street is a good place to hear up-and-coming artists while the Sugar Club on Leeson Street is a plush and stylish spot for all sorts of live music from jazz and blues to Latin. Other good venues for gigs include Crawdaddy (Hatch Street Upper) and Vicar Street (Vicar Street). Jazz fans should check out one of the city's oldest jazz venues JJ Smyth's (Aungier Street) with nightly gigs.

Dance

Dublin has a number of modern dance and ballet companies that perform at various venues. For traditional Irish dancing, go to **O'Shea's Merchant** *(see page 82)*. **Cultúrlann na hÉireann** holds concerts, stage shows and traditional dances in Monkstown (tel: 280 0295).

Film

O'Connell Street is the main city centre location for the big new-release cinemas, including the historical **Savoy Cinema**. Art-house and international films are shown at the **Irish Film Centre**, in Eustace Street. The centre contains the National Film Archive, and its two cinemas present a varied programme of new international and archival films. The **Screen** in D'Olier Street also shows international films. In summer, open-air movies are screened in Meeting House Square in Temple Bar.

Nightclubs

As in every other city, nightclubs quickly come and go, so it is essential to check the listings in local publications like *In Dublin* or *Events*.

A night on the town

Leeson Street was always a popular spot for late-night dance clubs, but its popularity is on the wane and the 'strip' is now dotted with lap-dancing clubs although some of the old Leeson Street stalwarts like Legs still remain. Dublin's beautiful people flock to Renards (South Frederick Street) and Lillies Bordello (Adam Court, Grafton Street), but they both have a relatively strict door policy. Spy Nightclub (Powerscourt Townhouse) is sleek, loud and buzzing, while the newest place to be seen is Krystal on Harcourt Street.

SPORTS

Golf

Golf is extremely popular, and there are many superb courses in and around Dublin. The Royal Golf Club at Dollymount and many other clubs welcome visitors; booking is rarely required. For further information, contact Dublin Tourism or the **Golfing Union of Ireland** (tel: 269 4111).

Pier fishing is well signposted and doesn't require a licence

Fishing

Sea angling is permitted all year, but river fishing requires a licence. Information can be obtained from Dublin Tourism or any fishing shop.

Spectator Sports

The traditional Irish games of **hurling** and **Gaelic football** are played at Croke Park. **Horse racing** takes place at Leopardstown; and at the Curragh (flat racing) and Punchestown (National Hunt racing) in County Kildare. The premiere **show jumping** event is the Kerrygold Horse Show at the RDS. **Greyhound racing** is on at Shelbourne Park, Ringsend, and at Harold's Cross Stadium. **Rugby** and **football** (soccer) are played at Lansdowne Road in Ballsbridge.

Watersports/Beaches

Although there are beaches at Malahide and Dollymount, the very best ones are in the south, at Bray and Killiney. At Sandycove there's the **Forty Foot** bathing spot, which was once a men's nude beach, but is now open to everyone. It is not advisable to swim within 8km (5 miles) of the city centre because of pollution.

DUBLIN FOR CHILDREN

There are plenty of things for children to enjoy in Dublin. Note that family tickets are available for rail and bus services and that children under 16 travel at half-fare on buses and DART.

The Ark, on Eustace Street in Temple Bar, is a children's cultural centre that offers a changing programme of plays, workshops, readings and performances, all geared towards youngsters. It's best to book in advance for the activities, as The Ark has become quite popular, and activities sometimes fill up in advance (tel: 670 7788). The well-loved **Lambert Puppet Theatre** in Monkstown stages panto-style plays geared for young audiences.

Museums that will appeal to children include the **Fry Model Railway Museum** at Malahide Castle and Estate *(see page 77)* and the **National Wax Museum** which relocated to Grafton Street in 2007. There are nature trails in **Phoenix Park** and the **Dublin Zoo** has a pet corner and zoo train especially designed for younger children *(see pages 66–7)*.

A popular children's attraction

Older children should enjoy **Dublinia** *(see page 43)*, a lively re-creation of medieval 'Diflin', while the self-guided **Rock 'n' Stroll Trail** around Dublin, which follows in the footsteps of Irish rock legends, should appeal particularly to the teenage crowd.

Festivals and Events

As dates frequently change, we advise you to contact the Irish National Tourist Board or Dublin Tourism Centre *(see page 126)* for up-to-date information on particular festivals.

February/March Rugby Six Nations Championships: Landsdowne Road, Ballsbridge. Dublin International Film Festival, various cinemas.

March St Patrick's Day Parade: marching bands from all over the world and live music in a festive atmosphere.

April Handel's Messiah commemorative concert on the 13th – the anniversary of its premiere in 1742 – Temple Bar. International Dance Festival Ireland: various venues, a range of contemporary dance performances from top companies around the world.

June Bloomsday: Dublin city centre. Celebration of Joyce and *Ulysses* in city streets and parks, and at the Joyce Museum, Sandycove. Bloom: a flower-show and gardening extravaganza held in the Phoenix Park. Taste of Dublin: A four-day celebration of food and drink in the Iveagh Gardens. Street Performance World Championships: street performers from all over the world compete in Merrion Square.

July Oxegen Festival: various venues. This two-day rock festival is one of the biggest events on the Irish music calendar.

August Dublin Horse Show: RDS, Ballsbridge. International equestrian event. Dún Laoghaire Festival: parades, music, sports events. The Dun Laoghaire Festival of World Cultures: A fantastic celebration of global culture, music and dance.

September All-Ireland Hurling and Football Finals: Croke Park. Dublin Theatre Festival: Abbey and Gate theatres and other venues. Companies from all over the world, plus new Irish work. Bulmer's Comedy Festival: a riotous comedy festival with gigs in venues throughout the capital. Dublin Fringe Festival: offbeat sister to the main theatre festival with gigs in unusual venues including the Spiegeltent.

October Dublin City Marathon: a run through the historic streets.

December National Crafts Fair of Ireland: RDS, Ballsbridge. Leopardstown Christmas Racing Festival: a four-day festival at the end of December.

EATING OUT

The days of overcooked cabbage, mountains of boiled potatoes, and cholesterol-laden fried meat are long gone in Dublin. Not only is there a new Irish cuisine, created by imaginative young chefs, but ethnic restaurants of all kinds give a wider choice than ever before.

Of course, Dublin has always had the fresh ingredients for a fine cuisine. Situated as it is on the broad sweep of Dublin Bay, with the waters of the Atlantic nearby and a plethora of streams and rivers, the city has access to both sea and freshwater fish in abundance – succulent oysters, freshly caught lobster and crab, wild salmon, sole and pike. Tender lamb comes from Kerry and Wicklow; country cheeses, made on farms and in monasteries have begun to achieve a worldwide reputation. Irish breads, apple tarts and fruit cakes have always been delicious, and are still here. So are traditional Irish dishes, but prepared with greater delicacy and lightness of touch. And there are restaurants that cater for vegetarians.

Meals and Meal Times

Breakfast is either the 'continental' variety – fruit juice, bread, cereals, coffee or tea – or traditional Irish, which generally means robust portions of fried eggs, bacon, tomatoes and sausages, black pudding and bread, washed down with coffee or strong tea. Most hotels and restaurants serve breakfast from around 6 or 7am until about 10am.

Lunch is from around noon until 2.30 or 3pm. Many of the more expensive restaurants offer three- or four-course set lunches, but you can also find simple salads, sandwiches or hot meals at most pubs, cafés and snack-bars. Most cafés serve snacks and light meals all day from 8.30 or 9am until 6pm, though many stay open until as late as 1 or 2am.

Dinner hours usually begin around 6pm. Many restaurants offer an early pre-theatre dinner that's usually a good bargain. Fixed-price meals are often the best value.

WHERE TO EAT

The choice in Dublin ranges from elegant restaurants, often with French or Modern Irish cuisine, to the humble chip shop offering crispy batter-coated portions of tasty fish and chips (try the famous Leo Burdock's at 2 Werburgh Street, near the Castle). In between, there are pubs, bistros and moderately priced restaurants of all kinds. Dublin's restaurants range from those serving traditional dishes to Chinese, Creole, Indian, Indonesian, Japanese, Thai, vegetarian cuisine and more.

There are also cafés, self-service snack bars, and the usual fast-food places. Standards of service can vary considerably

The elegant Café en Seine, on Dawson Street

A bowl of Irish stew

from one place to the next, but most establishments are welcoming and friendly. Pubs and bars are a good choice for lunch. For our selection of places to eat, turn to page 136.

Important for the visitor are the often superior cafés and restaurants in museums, great houses and other attractions. They offer everything from pastries and snacks to hot meals with wine. A nice spot is the Irish Film Centre, in the Temple Bar district. Another excellent café-restaurant is in the intimate vaulted basement of the Irish Museum of Modern Art, while the National Gallery museum café (an outlet of Fitzer's) is also good and stays open until 8pm on Thursday.

Cafés and Tearooms

While Dublin's abandonment of tea in favour of coffee is wholesale, the Dublin traditional high tea is still going strong in the city's grand hotels such as the Shelbourne, Westbury and the Gresham. To the background strains of soothing Irish harp or piano music, a liveried waiter will bring you a pot of freshly brewed tea and a silver tray laden with dainty, delicious-looking sandwiches, scones, sweet cakes and pastries.

Dublin is full of cafés where you can get an excellent cup of coffee (and tea if you must) along with a pastry, or a more substantial meal. Cafés also provide some of the best places to sit and watch the world rush by. Gloria Jean's, on South William Street, serves a formidable cup of coffee. There are plenty of delicatessens and sandwich bars that cater for the quick-business-lunch trade, and many of these are very good indeed.

WHAT TO EAT

Starters and Main Courses

It's no surprise that **fish** and **seafood** figure largely on Dublin menus. Wild Irish salmon tops the list. It can be poached, roasted or steamed, and is generally served simply with light sauces or just a slice of lemon. Alternatively, smoked salmon is a popular choice and is served thinly sliced as a starter or with scrambled eggs as a brunch dish. Salmon gravalax is currently a stylish starter in restaurants around Dublin.

Dublin Bay prawns are also very popular as a starter. However you choose to eat them, they are always plump, juicy and delicious. Galway Bay oysters are scrumptious – best with a pint of Guinness. A variety of freshwater fish, mussels from Wexford (try the mussel soup), Donegal crab, West Cork King Scallops and Dingle Bay lobster complete the list.

Traditional Fare

Traditional Irish dishes are now being re-worked for a younger market. Some old-fashioned dishes to look for include *colcannon* (mashed potatoes with leeks and cabbage), *crubeens* (pigs' trotters), *coddle* (boiled bacon, sausages, onions and potatoes), *boxty* (a tasty potato pancake filled with meat, vegetables or fish), Dublin Lawyer (lobster, flamed in whiskey and simmered in cream) and, of course, the traditional Irish stew, made with lamb, potatoes and vegetables.

As is common in restaurants around the world, **meat** on the menu in Irish restaurants is generally served simply to allow the fine flavour to speak for itself. The lamb in Ireland is of the highest quality and features frequently on city menus in guises such as herb crusted rack of lamb. Irish beef is also a favourite, with prime Irish rib eyes and roasted fillet served with elegant sauces, seasonal vegetables and fondant potatoes. Venison is another popular choice at quality restaurants, as is rabbit or hare. Pork also features strongly, from roast belly of pork to herb-accented gourmet sausages served simply with mash. Home-raised free-range or organic chicken is full of flavour.

Vegetarians are particularly well catered for in Dublin. There are quite a few specialist and semi-specialist vegetarian places, and often you'll have a choice between dishes like vegetable couscous, or parsnips stuffed with brazil nuts and vegetables in a red pepper sauce or the unspectacular, though equally delicious, tagliatelle with mushrooms and tomatoes – the many Italian restaurants are always good for vegetarian options. Cornucopia on Wicklow Street is strictly vegetarian and serves such a variety of tasty daily specials, you may decide not to eat anywhere else while in the capital.

Bread, Pastries and Desserts

You could find wonderful freshly baked Irish breads even in the old boiled-potato days. Unfortunately, the pseudo- croissant is now ubiquitous, but happily so are soda bread, wholemeal bread, and all manner of scrumptious scones. Old-fashioned classic Irish confections like porter cake and barmbrack are also still around.

Whatever your choice of dessert, you will usually be asked if you want cream with it. Irish cream is thick and delicious, particularly when served with apple tart. Dessert cakes, puddings, and ice-cream dessert combinations tend to be sweet and rich, so be prepared for a major test of your dietary resolve.

Drinks

Dublin wouldn't be Dublin without the world-famous stout, Guinness, which really does taste better here than anywhere else. The pouring and settling process takes a little time, but it's worth the wait. Murphy's and other Irish stouts are also wonderful. Don't miss the range of brews now available from microbreweries.

There is also a great array of distinctive Irish whiskeys – you'll see their names etched in the glass of pub windows. Wine is readily available everywhere, with a fine selection of Australian cabernets and chardonnays, and Chilean wines. Light Italian reds also feature prominently on wine lists. The cheapest way to order wine is to ask for a carafe of the house wine with your meal. Remember that VAT is charged on wine. It's generally cheaper in Dublin to drink in pubs rather than hotel bars. Prices are highest in the city centre.

A Bloomsday sampling of one of Ireland's best exports

HANDY TRAVEL TIPS

An A–Z Summary of Practical Information

A

ACCOMMODATION *(See also YOUTH HOSTELS and the selection of RECOMMENDED HOTELS starting on page 128)*

Hotels in Ireland are classified by star ratings from one to five stars, and are registered and regularly inspected by the Irish Tourist Board (Bord Fáilte). The Tourist Board also publishes a list of approved hotel and guesthouse accommodation throughout Dublin, obtainable through your local tourist information office (see Tourist Information). Hotel information can also be found on the Irish Hotels Federation website <www.irelandhotels.com>.

All tourism information offices operate an accommodation reservation service, for which a small charge is made. It is always advisable to book accommodation in advance, especially if you plan to visit in the peak months of July and August.

Hotels generally offer a full range of services, including restaurants, licensed bars, currency exchange offices, gift shops and lounges, while **guesthouses** provide more limited facilities, but are excellent value. Be aware that room prices quoted normally include the government tax (VAT) of 13.5 percent but do not always include service charges, which will add an extra 10 to 15 percent to your bill. Breakfast is often extra. Ask when you book. If a room is referred to as 'en suite', it means that the room has a private bath.

Details about **self-catering accommodation** in Dublin and the surrounding area can be obtained from the Irish Tourist Board (which produces a complete illustrated guide). Dublin also offers a variety of college and **university accommodation** when classes are not being held. Rooms and apartments at bargain rates are available on the Trinity College campus between June and September. For further information, contact the Accommodation Office, Trinity College, Dublin 2, tel: 608 1177; fax: 671 1267; <www.tcd.ie>. University College Dublin provides a similar service. For further information, contact Accommodation Office, UCD, Belfield, Dublin 4, tel: 716 1034; fax: 716 1154; <www.ucd.ie>. Details of student accommodation can be obtained from the Student Travel Services, 19 Aston Quay, Dublin 2, tel: 602 1777.

Holiday Hostels provide simple accommodation in dormitory-style rooms or shared bedrooms for visitors on a tight budget and are open all year. For details of hostels in Dublin, contact the Irish Tourist Board. Three places you can contact directly are:

Avalon House, Budget Accommodation Centre, 55 Aungier Street, Dublin 2, tel: 475 0001; fax: 475 0303; <www.avalon-house.ie>.

Kinlay House Dublin, Accommodation Centre, 2–12 Lord Edward Street, Dublin 2, tel: 679 6644; fax: 679 7437; <www.kinlayhouse.ie>.

Independent Holiday Hostels, tel: 836 4700; <www.hostels-ireland.com>.

AIRPORTS

Dublin International Airport is 11km (7 miles) north of the city centre. It offers a range of facilities, including a duty-free shopping centre, tourism information office, bank, bureau de change, post office, and branches of the major car hire firms. The airport is managed by Aer Rianta (information line tel: 814 1111).

The airport is serviced by bus and taxi. **Airlink**, a regular shuttle service connecting it to the city centre is operated by Dublin Bus <www.dublinbus.ie>. Buses leave from outside the Arrivals Hall and connect with the central bus station (Busáras), railway stations (Heuston Station, Connolly Rail/DART station) and the city centre. Buses leave every 10–15 minutes from 5.45am until 11.30pm; buy tickets from the bus driver. **Aircoach** <www.aircoach.ie> operates a competing 24-hour service with buses leaving every 10 minutes from 6am–8pm and less frequently after that. A cheaper option, if you have plenty of time, is to take city buses 41, 41B, 747 or 748 to the city centre. An **Air DART** bus takes people the short way to Howth Junction DART Station. From there you can access any station on the DART network. Taxis line up outside the Arrivals Terminal.

B

BUDGETING FOR YOUR TRIP

Dublin is relatively expensive compared to other European capitals, and accommodation and eating out can quickly eat into your budget. The following are given as a rough guide only:

Accommodation. A double room in a mid-range hotel in Dublin costs from about €100 upwards per room, but you're more likely to find most places hovering around the €150 mark. Five-star hotels can easily set you back three or four times this amount. There are plenty of inexpensive accommodation options if you're prepared to look around.

Meals and drinks. Stopping off for a coffee in Dublin can often be expensive at around €2 to €3 for a cappuccino or latte. Drinks in bars and pubs are expensive and nowhere more so than in hotels. In city centre pubs you'll pay around €5 for a pint of lager, while a spirit and a mixer can set you back around €7. Guinness usually costs from around €4 a pint. There are a wide range of restaurants and cafes available from cheaply priced noodle bars like Wagamama to Michelin-starred establishments. Most restaurants are mid-range with main courses around €20 and upwards.

Entertainment. Cinema tickets costs around €10 depending on location, time and your status; admission to a nightclub is €10 and more. Many museums and galleries have free admission making sightseeing a relatively cheap option, although attractions like the Guinness Storehouse can be pricey at €14 for an adult.

Transport. An adult rail only day ticket (short hop) costs €7.20; bus/rail costs €8.80 and Luas/rail costs €8.20. A three-day unlimited travel ticket costs €15.30 for rail only and €17.30 for bus/rail only.

Specials: The Dublin Pass ticket includes free entry to over 30 top visitor attractions, discounts to shops, restaurants, cafes, theatres, venues, tours, free transport to Dublin City with Aircoach from the airport, and an 84-page guidebook to Dublin. Dublin passes are available for 1,2,3 and 6 days. Prices starts at €31 for an adult day pass.

C

CAR HIRE *(See also DRIVING)*

It is worth hiring a car to explore the countryside around Dublin, although driving a car in the heavy city traffic is not advisable. You can arrange to hire a car immediately upon arrival at Dublin airport, or have one waiting for you if you book a fly-drive or rail-sail-drive inclusive package. Major car hire companies are represented at the airport, and there are many local firms listed in the Golden Pages of the telephone directory.

To hire a car you'll need a driving licence issued in your home country, valid for at least two to five years. The minimum age (usually 23–26 years) varies from company to company. Rates include third-party liability insurance, but collision damage waiver (CDW) must be paid for separately at about €10 per day. Personal accident insurance (PAI), theft insurance, and third party property damage (TPPD – without it the hirer will typically be responsible for the first €1,500 of damage) are also available, each costing about €5 per day. Road assistance is supplied by the Automobile Association (56 Drury Street, Dublin 2; Emergency Service, tel: 677 9481).

Major car hire companies:

Avis, Airport Arrivals Hall and 35–39 Old Kilmainham Road, Dublin 8, tel: 605 7500; <www.avis.ie>.
Budget, Airport Arrivals Hall and 151 Drumcondra Road Lower, Dublin 9, tel: 837 9611; <www.budgetcarrental.ie>.
Hertz, Airport Arrivals Hall, tel: 844 5466; <www.hertz.ie>.
National, Airport Arrivals Hall and Cranford Centre, Stillorgan, Dublin 4, tel: 260 3771; <www.carhire.ie>.
Argus, a local company, is at the airport and other city locations, tel: 490 4444; <www.argus-rentacar.com>.
Dan Dooley, another local company, is at the Airport Arrivals Hall and Westland Row, city centre, tel: 677 2723; <www.dan-dooley.ie>.

CLIMATE

Dublin's climate is temperate, without extremes of temperature, thanks to the warming Gulf Stream that influences much of the country. Due to blustery winds coming in from the Irish Sea the weather is unpredictable and can change very quickly from rain to sun (and vice versa). Less rain falls on Dublin than on any other part of the country, however, and snow is a rare occurrence. Summers can be quite cool, and days can be unexpectedly warm in winter.

	J	F	M	A	M	J	J	A	S	O	N	D
°C	7	8	11	13	16	18	20	21	17	14	11	8
°F	45	46	52	55	61	64	68	70	63	57	52	46

CLOTHING

Dubliners are fashion-conscious, and a certain standard of attire is expected in exclusive hotels and restaurants. Business people still dress in formal dark suits. For everyday wear, however, jeans and casual clothes are appropriate. A raincoat or umbrella are absolute necessities. If you plan to walk a lot, especially in the environs, bring sturdy shoes and a sweater: even if it looks like a glorious day, it can turn cold later on. Pack warm clothing for winter, and a jacket and sweater in summer. Evening temperatures on the sunniest summer days can be quite cool, and in spring there is often a chilling wind, which adds an edge to the day's mild warmth.

CRIME AND SAFETY (See also EMERGENCIES)

Compared to most urban centres, Dublin's crime rate is moderate, and violent street crime is rare. However, crime is unfortunately on the increase. Take sensible measures. Leave your valuables in the hotel safe, keep your wallet in an inside pocket or hang your bag strap across your chest. Be wary of pickpockets in pubs or crowded places, and don't flash your money around when using street side ATMs.

If you are robbed, report the incident to the hotel receptionist and the nearest police station, so that the police can provide you with a certificate to present to your insurance company. Call your consulate if your passport has been stolen. Tourist information offices and some attractions provide a multilingual leaflet produced by the Gardai (see also Police), entitled *A Short Guide to Tourist Security*. The Irish Tourist Assistance Service is there to help tourists who fall victim to crime. Opening hours are Mon–Sat 10am–6pm, Sun and holidays 12–6pm; tel: (01) 478 5295.

CUSTOMS AND ENTRY REQUIREMENTS

For a stay of up to three months in Ireland, a valid passport is sufficient for citizens of Australia, Canada, New Zealand, South Africa and the US. Visitors from European Union (EU) countries need only bring an identity card and are free to stay indefinitely in the country, and work if they wish.

Since Ireland is a member of the EU, free exchange of non-duty-free goods for personal use is permitted between Ireland and the continent. If you are from a non-EU country, you are still entitled to a duty-free allowance: 200 cigarettes, 50 cigars or 250g tobacco; 2 litres of wine and 1 litre of spirits; and 60ml perfume. Meat, meat products, vegetables, fruit and the like may not be brought into Ireland. Pornographic materials are also prohibited. There are no currency restrictions.

For residents of non-EU countries returning home, the allowances are: Australia: A$400 of goods, 250 cigarettes or 250g tobacco or 100 cigars; 1 litre spirits or wine; Canada: $500 of goods, 200 cigarettes and 50 cigars; 1 litre spirits or wine or 8.5 litres beer; New Zealand: NZ$700 of goods, 250g of tobacco products; 4.5 litres wine or beer and 1 litre spirits; South Africa: 400 cigarettes and 50 cigars and 250g tobacco; 2 litres wine and 1 litre spirits; US: $400 of goods, 200 cigarettes and 100 non-Cuban cigars or 2kg tobacco, 1 litre wine or spirits; antiques over 100 years old are also allowed.

D

DRIVING

Road Conditions. Rush-hour traffic jams and limited parking space make driving in central Dublin an unpleasant experience. Bottlenecks form rapidly on the city's narrow streets, especially in rush hours. If you must drive in the city centre, try and plan your journey between 10am and 4pm to avoid the worst congestion.

Outside the city is a motorway system for rapid transit, but most scenic routes, such as those through the Wicklow Mountains, tend to be narrow, winding and steep, with bad visibility and possible ice in winter. Road users in Ireland tend to take everyone's life in their hands: speeding and overtaking at heartstopping places – drive defensively.

Rules and Regulations. Traffic follows the same basic rules that apply in Britain. Drive on the left, overtake (pass) on the right. Turn left on a roundabout (traffic circle); at a junction where no road has priority, yield to traffic coming from the right. Road signs giving place directions are bilingual, in Irish and English, and distances are shown in kilometres. Seat belts in both the front and back must be worn, and children under 12 must travel in the rear. Ireland has very strict rules about drinking and driving – don't do it.

Petrol (gas). There are filling stations everywhere, many of them are self-service. A number are open 24 hours. Petrol is sold by the litre and comes in three grades: lead replacement petrol, unleaded and super unleaded.

Parking. It's almost impossible to find free parking on Dublin's streets during normal working hours, but you may have better luck at weekends. Expect to be towed away or heavily fined for parking illegally. Metered parking (for up to 2 hours) is quite limited. Your safest bet is to park in one of the multistorey car parks, which are not expensive: from €2.50 an hour, with a flat evening rate. Look for computerised signs giving information about availability.

Speed limits. The speed limit is 50 km/h in towns and cities, 80 km on regional and local roads and 110 km/h on national roads. On motorways the speed limit is 120 km/h.

If You Need Help. If you are a member of an AIT driving club or the AA, call the Automobile Association of Ireland: tel: 617 9540. The Royal Automobile Club (RAC) also has a breakdown number: tel: (toll-free) 800 535005.

E

ELECTRICITY

Ireland's electrical supply is 220 volts 50 cycles AC. Plugs are 3-pin flat or 2-pin round. If you need a travel adaptor, bring one with you.

EMBASSIES AND CONSULATES

Get in touch with the embassy/consulate of your home country if something disastrous happens – for example, if you lose your passport, get into trouble with the authorities or have an accident. The Consul can issue emergency passports, give advice on obtaining money from home, and provide a list of lawyers and doctors

Australia:	Fitzwilton House, Wilton Terrace, Dublin 2; tel: 664 5300; <www.australianembassy.ie>
Canada:	65 St Stephen's Green, Dublin 2, tel: 417 4100; <www.canadaeuropa.gc.ca/ireland/>
South Africa:	Earlsfort Centre, Dublin 2, tel: 661 5553.
UK:	29 Merrion Road, Dublin 4, tel: 205 3700; <www.britishembassy.ie>
US:	42 Elgin Road, Dublin 4, tel: 668 8777; <http://dublin.usembassy.gov>

EMERGENCIES (See also HEALTH AND MEDICAL CARE and POLICE)

In the event of an emergency, dial 999 or 112 for Police, Ambulance, Fire and Coastguard. The call is free from all pay- and card phones.

G

GAY AND LESBIAN TRAVELLERS

Legislation ending the laws that criminalised male homosexuality was only passed in 1993. The repeal of these laws has brought about many changes in the gay scene. Though still small, the gay and lesbian community is now both visible and welcoming to visitors. The monthly newspaper, *Gay Community News* <www.gcn.ic> is widely available, and there are listings and features in many of Dublin's free magazines and papers. Annual gay events are Mardi Gras (end of May), Pride (late June), and the Lesbian and Gay Film Festival (in the Irish Film Centre, end of July). Good bars and nightclubs include the long-standing George (South Great George's Street), The Front Lounge (Parliament Street), and Dragon (South Great George's Street).

   Help and information lines include Gay Switchboard Dublin, tel: 872 1055; Lesbian Line, tel: 872 9911. Outhouse (105 Capel Street, Dublin 2, tel: 873 4933; <www.outhouse.ie>) is a meeting place for the lesbian and gay community.

GETTING THERE (See also AIRPORTS)

By Air. Ireland's national airline is Aer Lingus <www.aerlingus.com>, which operates direct flights to Dublin from Boston/Logan, Chicago/ O'Hare, Newark, Los Angeles and New York/JFK and San Francisco in the US; and from Birmingham, Edinburgh, Glasgow, London/ Heathrow, Manchester and Newcastle in the UK; major air connections from the Continent include Amsterdam, Berlin, Brussels, Copenhagen, Frankfurt, Geneva, Madrid, Munich, Paris, Prague, Rome/da Vinci, Vienna and Warsaw. Ireland's other national airline, Ryanair <www.ryanair.com> operates budget flights to Dublin from London/

Gatwick/Luton/Stansted, Aberdeen, Birmingham, Blackpool, Bristol, Cardiff, Doncaster, Durham, Edinburgh, East Midlands, Glasgow Prestwick, Leeds, Liverpool and Manchester.

From the US there are also direct flights to Dublin on Continental from JFK and Newark; and on Delta from Atlanta. Visitors flying from Australia, Canada or New Zealand must make connections through London or another British hub with Aer Lingus, British Airways, British Midlands or Ryanair. Connections can also be made through another European hub: Air France, Lufthansa and Alitalia fly to Dublin. Slatterys Travel operates flights between Dublin and South Africa <www.slatterys.com>.

There is a wide range of special promotional fares to Ireland (Ryanair offers many inexpensive fares to Britain), and discounts are available for senior citizens and students holding a valid International Student Identity Card. The cheapest fares on regular flights are APEX (advance purchase excursion) and super APEX, which must be booked and paid for three to four weeks in advance.

Packages that include a hotel room generally offer the best rates and conditions. A wide range of package tours or special-interest holidays are available, including fly-drive, sporting and activity holidays, and short breaks.

By Bus. Bus services linking Britain and Dublin are operated by Bus Eireann <www.buseireann.ie>, Ireland's national bus company (Travel Centre, Busáras, Store Street, Dublin 1, tel: 836 6111), in conjunction with Eurolines <www.eurolines.ie> via Dublin Ferryport and Dun Laoghaire upon Stena Line or Irish Ferries. Routes connect London and other major British towns to Dublin's central bus station, Busáras. Most routes run daily, but some are seasonal so you should contact your travel agent for the latest information.

Countrywide bus services throughout Ireland are also provided by Bus Éireann. Departures are from Busáras (the central bus station), located in Store Street.

By Ferry. There are two main ferry companies. Irish Ferries runs ships from Dublin Port to Holyhead (tel: (0818) 300 400 for information and reservations in Ireland, tel: (08705) 171717 in the UK, <www.irishferries.com>); Stena Sealink operates boats from the Ferry Terminal in Dun Laoghaire to Holyhead. They offer both a regular service and a high-speed service that takes about half the normal time. For Stena Sealink reservations and information in Ireland, tel: 204 7777; in the UK, tel: (08705) 707070; <www.stenaline.co.uk>. Irish Ferries also sails from Rosslare to Le Havre and Cherbourg.

GUIDED TOURS

Bus Tours. City sightseeing tours by bus provide an excellent introduction to Dublin. Dublin Bus (59 Upper O'Connell Street, Dublin 1, tel: 873 4222; <www.dublinbus.ie>) operates a city tour that takes in the principal sights; in good weather, the tour is by open-top bus. The tour guides are entertaining, you can hop on or off at any of the stops, and your ticket is valid all day. Irish City Tours tel: 605 7705; <www.irishcitytours.com> has a similar service, with tickets available on the bus. Dublin Bus also has an amusing, offbeat Ghost Bus Tour in the evening.

Bus Éireann runs day trips out of the city to sights such as Glendalough, Newgrange and the Boyne Valley, Russborough House and Powerscourt Gardens, as well as further afield. All tours depart from the Travel Centre at Busáras *(see page 114)*. Gray Line Tours (Dublin Tourism Centre, Suffolk Street, Dublin 2, tel: 605 7705) offers a similar range of excursions. Tours depart from the Gray Line desk at the Dublin Tourism Centre and from a number of hotels.

Walking Tours. Dublin Tourism has signposted three self-guided walking tours, which you can enjoy at your own speed. The Cultural Heritage Trail covers Dublin north of the Liffey, while the Old City Heritage Trail heads east from Trinity College through Temple Bar to Dublin Castle. The Georgian Heritage Trail focuses on the city south of the river around St Stephen's Green, Fitzwilliam and Merrion Squares, and includes the National Gallery, National Museum and National Library. The Rock'n'Stroll Trail, for music fans, points out places associated with such artists as Bob Geldof, U2, Sinead O'Connor and the Chieftains, among others. Dublin Tourism also publishes The Dublin Touring Guide, with walks around the city and excursions on public transport. The Dublin Tourism website contains a series of iWalks (<www.visitdublin.com/iwalks>), which are audio guides that can be downloaded onto an iPod or MP3 player.

The enjoyable Dublin Literary Pub Crawl, comprises an evening of readings, song and performance following in the footsteps of James Joyce, Samuel Beckett, Brendan Behan and others, tel: 670 5602; <www.dublinpubcrawl.com> or book at the Dublin Tourism Centre. Historical Walking Tours of Dublin have walks on various themes from architecture to Vikings, tel: 878 0227; <www.historicalinsights.ie>. The Traditional Irish Musical Pub Crawl is led by a couple of professional musicians – they play and sing and talk about the history of Irish music. You can book at the Tourism Centre or contact Discover Dublin, tel: 475 3313; <www.discoverdublin.ie>.

Book direct or through the Tourism Centre for the Literary/Georgian Walk, run by Dublin Footsteps, tel: 496 0641, which takes in the highlights of Dublin's literary locations and Georgian architecture.

The International Bar on Wicklow Street is the starting point for the daily 1916 Rebellion Walking Tour taking in sights of the Easter Rising. To book, tel: (086) 8 583 847; <www.1916rising.com>. A Ghostly tour begins outside Dublin Castle every evening. The Zozimus Ghostly Experience visits the scenes of murders and myths. Tel: 661 8646; <www.zozimus.com/touringinfo.htm>.

Wet and Dry Tour. Viking Splash Tours, tel: 707 6000; <www.vikingsplash.ie>, depart from Bull Alley (beside St Patrick's Cathedral Park) and St Stephen's Green North in a vehicle that takes you along the canals and rivers of Dublin as well as the streets.

There are many other tours available. You'll find more information at the Dublin Tourism Centre in Suffolk Street, and most outings can be booked there.

H

HEALTH AND MEDICAL CARE

Visitors who are not covered by their medical insurance should take out a short-term holiday policy before setting out: US citizens should note that Medicare does not cover them while they are abroad. Citizens of EU countries are covered by a reciprocal agreement and may use the Irish health services for medical treatment and hospital stays. British visitors should make sure they have an European Health Insurance Card (EHIC), available from post offices or online.

In the event of an accident, dial 999 or 112 for an ambulance. Your hotel or guesthouse proprietor will contact a doctor in an emergency. You can also contact the Irish Medical Organisation at 10 Fitzwilliam Place, Dublin 2, tel: 676 7273 for a recommendation. Beaumont Hospital, Beaumont Road, Dublin 9, tel: 809 3000, has a 24-hour emergency room. For non-emergency services, try the Grafton Street Centre on Grafton Street, tel: 671 2122.

If you need emergency dental treatment, call the Irish Dental Association, 10 Richview Office Park, Clonskeagh Road, Dublin 14; tel: 295 0072, which will be able to recommend a dentist.

Pharmacies (drugstores) are generally open during normal business hours. You can find the address of the nearest late-night pharmacy in the local press and under 'Chemists – Pharmaceutical' in the phone directory. There is a branch of Boots Chemists on Grafton Street. Chemists on O'Connell Street tend to stay open quite late.

HOLIDAYS

Shops, banks, official departments and restaurants are closed on public holidays. If a holiday falls on a Sunday, the following Monday is normally taken instead. Although Good Friday is not officially a public holiday, it is observed as such in most of Ireland and pubs are closed on that day.

1 January	New Year's Day
17 March	St Patrick's Day
25 December	Christmas Day
26 December	St Stephen's Day
Movable Dates	
March/April	Good Friday/Easter Monday
First Monday in June	Whit or June Holiday
First Monday in August	Summer BankHoliday
Last Monday in October	All Souls

I

INTERNET CAFÉS

Internet cafes can be tricky to find in Dublin and many have closed down in recent years. You shouldn't have to pay over e4 per hour. Central Cyber Café is conveniently located at 6 Grafton Street, above Bus Stop Newsagents, but expensive. The Global Internet Cafe is equally overpriced, but is centrally located on O'Connell Street and provides left luggage facilities and phone cards.

L

LANGUAGE

Ireland is officially bilingual, as you'll see from the signs, and on official occasions either English or Irish may be used. English is spoken in Dublin and throughout most of Ireland; Irish is the main language in the areas designated as *Gaeltacht*. However, Irish is a required school subject, so most Irish people have knowledge of it. Signs around Dublin are usually self-explanatory. On buses, *An Lár* means 'City Centre.'

M

MAPS

For detailed maps of Dublin and the area around it, try the *Dublin Street Atlas and Guide*, available in bookstores, or buy a similar mini-atlas. If you need less detail, the tourism office gives out, free, *The Dublin Map*: useful as all attractions are plotted on it.

MEDIA

Radio and TV. The national broadcasting authority is RTE *(Radio Telefís Éireann)* which runs several TV channels, RTE1 and RTE 2, and three radio stations, RTE1, 2FM, and Lyric FM. TG4 is a television station with programmes in Irish. There are also two independent stations, TV3 and Channel 6. Television programmes from Britain via the BBC and ITV (independent television) are available, as well as all the BBC radio stations. Many hotels are equipped to receive satellite television or cable via CNN, Sky TV and other operators.

Newspapers and Magazines. The *Irish Times* is the leading national daily, with interesting articles and a useful Notices section. The *Irish Independent* has more Ireland-focused coverage and publishes a special Sunday edition. The *Evening Herald*, hawked at numerous street corners, is Dublin's local tabloid, with an extensive *Classifieds* section, and in the mornings watch out for Herald AM and Metro which are given out free at DART stations. Most newsagents stock the main UK national dailies, plus the Irish edition of London's *Sunday Times*, and many sell American and European newspapers. Foreign newspapers and periodicals can be purchased at Easons, located at 40–42 Lower O'Connell Street.

For what's going on, try *In Dublin* and *Totally Dublin*, events listings magazines. The glossy magazine *The Dubliner* is a good bet for Dublin-focussed articles and restaurant reviews. Irish Tourism has several free publications.

MONEY

Currency. Ireland's monetary unit is the euro (€), which is divided into 100 cent (¢).
Coins: 1¢, 2¢, 5¢, 10¢, 20¢, 50¢, €1 and €2.
Notes: €5, €10, €20, €50 and €100.

Changing money. For the best exchange rate, visitors should use banks, post offices and bureaux de change. The best rates are often obtained by using a credit card. Note that the Bank of Ireland ATMs charge for transactions with foreign banks.

Credit cards and travellers' cheques. Credit cards are accepted in most hotels, restaurants, petrol stations and large shops. Some guesthouses may not accept credit cards, so be sure to ask before booking. Travellers' cheques, supported by identification, can be exchanged at most banks or main travel service offices.

OPENING HOURS

Banks are usually open 10am–4pm Monday–Friday and 10am–5pm on Thursday; nearly all are open at lunchtime. Later closing times are gradually being introduced throughout Ireland.

Some shops follow Dublin's normal opening hours: Monday–Saturday 9/9.30am–5.30/6pm, with late-night shopping on Thursday until 8pm. A few suburban shopping centres stay open until 9pm on Thursday or Friday. In tourist areas hours are usually extended, and most places in Grafton Street remain open well into the evening and on Sunday. Many small groceries have late night opening and there are a few 24-hour shops in inner suburbs such as Rathmines/Ranelagh in the south and Phibsboro/Cabra in the north.

Most pubs are open all day from 10.30am until 12.30am, with a slightly later opening on Sunday, and earlier closing in winter.

P

POLICE

The emergency number for the Gardai is 999 or 112. Garda Headquarters is at 2 Hanover Street, Dublin 2, tel: 666 0000.

POST OFFICES

Post office branches are open Monday–Friday 9am–5.30pm, and Saturday 9am–1pm. There is a post office at Dublin Airport, and a convenient branch is off Grafton Street on South Anne Street. Mailboxes are painted green and have the word 'Post' in yellow on the top.

Dublin's main post office is the General Post Office (GPO) in O'Connell Street. It is open 8am–8pm Monday–Saturday and for stamps only on Sunday 10.30am–6pm. Many post offices exchange foreign currency and travellers' cheques.

PUBLIC TRANSPORT

Bus. The city's bus network is operated by Dublin Bus (Bus Átha Cliath), which is a subsidiary of the national transport company, CIE. The head office is at 59 O'Connell Street, Dublin 1 (tel: 873 4222 <www.dublinbus.ie>). Their green single- and double-deckers serve the city and the Greater Dublin area. Services include CitySwift (white and blue single-decker buses) and Imp (yellow and red minibuses) on some routes. Buses run from 6am–11.30pm. On popular routes, buses run every 10–20 minutes, but service on other routes could be much less frequent. There is a special hourly Nitelink service to the suburbs from 12.30–3.30am Thursday, Friday and Saturday (buses depart from College, D'Olier and Westmoreland streets every hour; buy your tickets from the van on College Street). A frequent bus service links Heuston Station and Busáras with Dublin airport. You need to have the right change ready unless you have a special pass *(see below)*, which should be inserted into the validator as you enter the bus on the right hand side (combined bus/DART tickets should be shown to the driver/conductor). If you over pay, the driver will print you a credit slip. Collect these and they will refund your money at the headquarters on O'Connell Street.

Fares. There are no flat fares on public transport, and the amount you pay depends on where you want to go. A range of discount passes are valid for bus or combined bus-and-rail. The one-day adult bus ticket allows unlimited travel for one day on all Dublin Bus services (except Nitelink). The one-day and three-day short-hop bus/rail tickets allow unlimited transport on Dublin Bus and DART for one person (except on Nitelink), while the family one-day ticket extends the same concessions to two adults and up to four children under 16. Combination bus and Luas tram tickets are also available. Seven-day passes are also available for unlimited travel on the bus, including the Airlink service. There are also a variety of student and children's passes. Passes can be obtained from the Dublin Bus booking office at 59 O'Connell Street or from any bus ticket agent.

Luas Tram. The Luas tram (tel: 1800 300 604, <www.luas.ie>) is Dublin's new Light Rail Transit system, connecting the city centre with outlying suburbs. There are two lines that operate weekdays 5.30am–12.00am, Sat 6.30am–12.30am, Sun 7am–11.30pm. The Red Line runs from Connolly Station to Tallaght every 10 minutes, with stops at Four Courts, Smithfield, the National Museum and Heuston Station. The Green Line runs from St Stephen's Green to Sandyford every 5–15 minutes. Single fares range from €1.40 to €2.10 depending on the distance travelled. All stops have ticket machines. Return tickets, one-day and seven-day tickets are also available.

Rail/DART. Dublin Area Rapid Transit (DART) provides a swift and efficient electrified rail link through the city, from the seaside towns of Howth in the north and Greystones in the south. The line runs along the Dublin Bay coast and serves a total of 28 stations. Trains run approximately every 15 minutes (every 5 minutes during rush hours) 7am–midnight Monday–Saturday, and 9.30am–11pm Sunday. Avoid travelling at peak times when trains are packed with commuters. Single fares range from €1.20 to €3.70.

Taxi. You'll find taxis at one of the many clearly marked taxi ranks located outside major hotels, bus and railway stations, and on busy thoroughfares. Taxis don't normally cruise for business. There are 24-hour taxi ranks at Aston Quay, College Green, O'Connell Street, Eden Quay, and St Stephen's Green (East and North). At busy times there can be a long wait. You can also order a taxi by calling a specific company; look in the Golden Pages of the telephone directory under 'Taxicabs'. You will probably have to pay a pick-up charge if you order a taxi by phone.

Taxis are identified by a sign giving the name of the firm and their number on the car roof. Rates are fixed by law and displayed in all taxis. They are valid for a 16-km (10-mile) radius outside the city; beyond that, fares should be negotiated in advance with the driver.

R

RELIGION

Ireland is predominantly a Roman Catholic country, but other religions are represented in Dublin. For a list of services, look in the Saturday edition of the *Irish Times*.

Roman Catholic. Pro-Cathedral, Marlborough Street, tel: 874 5441.
Church of Ireland. Christ Church Cathedral, Edward Square; tel: 677 8099. St Patrick's Cathedral, Patrick Street, tel: 475 4817.
Methodist. Dublin Central Mission, Abbey Street, tel: 874 0691.
Muslim. Mosque and Islamic Centre, 163 South Circular Road, Dublin 8, tel: 453 3242.
Unitarian. Unitarian Church, 112 St Stephen's Green West, Dublin 2, tel: 478 0638.

T

TELEPHONES

The telephone dialling code for the Dublin area when calling from outside the city is 01; the code for Ireland is 353. In this book, numbers within Dublin are listed minus the code. The Irish telephone operator is called Eircom. Direct-dial local and international calls can be made from all hotels and most guesthouses or from any public phone. Bear in mind that any calls made from a hotel will have a hefty surcharge.

To make a call within Dublin, dial only the seven-digit number. To call Dublin from elsewhere in Ireland, dial the 01 area code plus the seven-digit number. To reach Northern Ireland, dial 048, the area code, and the number. The access number for international calls is 00, followed by the country code: 61 for Australia, 64 for New Zealand, 27 for South Africa, 44 for the UK, and 1 for the US. Pay-phone international calls are cheaper after 6pm Mon–Fri and at any time over the weekend.

Though there are still some coin phones, telephone calling cards are widely used; you can buy them in units of 10, 20, 50 or 100 from post offices, newsstands or shops displaying a phone card notice. To use a phone card, listen for the dial tone, insert the card in the direction of the arrow, and dial the number. A display will show you how many units are left on the card, and when your card runs out, you will hear a beeping sound. To make a call on a coin phone, dial the number first, and wait until you are connected before you put in the coins. Note that mobile (cell) phones from the US will not work in Ireland.

To call directory enquiries for Ireland, dial 11811; for British and other international calls, dial 11818. This service isn't free, but you are entitled to make up to three inquiries per call. For an international operator, dial 114; for a local or British operator, dial 10.

If you need to make a lot of calls, Eircom has retail outlets on O'Connell Street and on King Street near Grafton where you can make calls from comfortable indoor facilities.

TICKETS

The Dublin Tourism Centre in Suffolk Street will book tickets to theatre, concerts and other events. Also contact Ticketmaster, tel: 0818 719 300; <www.ticketmaster.ie>. The following accept credit card bookings: Andrews Lane Theatre, tel: 679 5720; the Gaiety, tel: 677 1717; the Gate, tel: 874 4045; and the Olympia, tel: 679 3323.

TIME ZONES

Ireland follows Greenwich Mean Time (GMT: 1 hour earlier than Central European Time) from November to March and summer time (the same as Britain) from April to October. Ireland's latitude means that summer days are long (it's light until around 11pm), and that daylight hours in mid-winter are quite short (it's dark by 3.30pm).

New York	**Dublin**	Paris	Jo'burg	Sydney
7am	**noon**	1pm	2pm	10pm

TIPPING

Hotel bills usually include a service charge. If a service charge is included in a restaurant bill, tipping is not obligatory unless service has been exceptional. If you're unsure whether a service charge has been added, ask; if not, give 10–12 percent. Give your hairdresser/barber about 10–12 percent; porters e1–2 per bag; taxi drivers 10–12 percent.

TOILETS

Dublin is not well provided with public conveniences. Around Grafton Street, the shopping centres and Marks & Spencer have toilets on their top floors; there are toilets downstairs in the Trinity College Arts Building inside the Nassau Street gate. Use the facilities in museums, department stores or pubs. Toilets may be labelled with symbols, or with the words *Fir* for men and *Mna* for women.

TOURIST INFORMATION

Before you leave home, you can get information from the Irish National Tourist Board – **Bord Fáilte** (literally 'Board of Welcomes'), which maintains offices throughout the world. The main office is at Baggot Street Bridge, Dublin 2, tel: 602 4000; <www.ireland.ie>.

Australia: 36 Carrington Street, Sydney NSW 2000, tel: (02) 9299 6177

Canada: 2 Bloor Street West, Suite 3403, Toronto, Ontario M4W 3E2, tel: (1-800) 223 6470

New Zealand: 6th floor, 18 Shortland Street, Private Bag 92136, Auckland 1, tel: (09) 379 8720

UK: Tourism Ireland, Nations House, 103 Wigmore Street, London W1U 1QS, tel: (0800) 039 7000

US: 345 Park Avenue, New York, NY 10154, tel: (800) 223 6470

When you arrive in Dublin, your first stop should be the **Dublin Tourism Centre**, in Suffolk Street, Dublin 2, tel: 605 7700; <www.visitdublin.com>, located in the renovated St Andrews church. They have a bureau de change, a car hire agency, a desk for transport information, a café and a gift/bookshop. They can book tours, theatre and concert tickets, and accommodation (for a small charge), and have a wealth of brochures and other information. The centre is open all year Mon–Sat 9am–5.30pm (until 7pm Jul–Aug) Sun 10.30am–3pm.

Other locations are at the following addresses: Arrivals Building, Dublin International Airport (open: daily 8am–10pm); 14 Upper O'Connell Street, Dublin 2 (open Mon–Sat 9am–5pm); Dun Laoghaire Ferry Terminal (open: Mon–Sat 10am–1pm and 2–6pm).

TRAVELLERS WITH DISABILITIES

Most historic buildings and museums do not provide wheelchair access. An accommodation guide and fact sheets which indicate where wheelchair access and other facilities can be obtained for free from the Irish Tourist Board. Another useful contact is the National Disability Authority, tel: 608 0400; <www.nda.ie>.

WEBSITES

Information on the web can help you get ready for your trip to Dublin. There are many sites where you can find deals on airfares, hotels and car hire: <www.expedia.com> also has sites in Australia, Canada, and the UK; if you're travelling from the US try <www.bestfares.com> and <www.travelocity.com>. You can make hotel guesthouse or B&B reservations at <www.goireland.com>. The Irish Hotels Federation has a site at <www.irelandhotels.com>.

For sightseeing and other general information: <www.discoverireland.ie> is the excellent site of the Irish Tourist Board with international links on <www.discoverireland.com>; Dublin Tourism's site is <www.visitdublin.com>. Dúchas, the Heritage Services, also has a site: <www.heritageireland.ie>. To see what's going on try <www. entertainmentireland.ie> or the *Irish Times* at <www.ireland.com>.

WEIGHTS AND MEASURES

Ireland transferred to the metric system some time ago, although there are still hangovers from the past: milk comes in pints as well as litres, and cars tend to have speedometers in miles rather than in kilometres, although speed limits are in kms.

YOUTH HOSTELS

Members of the Independent Holiday Hostels of Ireland operate 19 hostels in and around Dublin. Many are open all year, and provide storage lockers, information desks, laundry facilities and bike hire as well as accommodation. The headquarters are at 57 Lower Gardiner Street, tel: 836 4700; fax: 836 4710; <www.hostels-ireland.com>.

Recommended Hotels

There is sometimes little difference between hotels and guesthouses, but the latter are usually cheaper, and city centre hotels, especially in Temple Bar, tend to be more noisy.

Listed below is a selection of hotels in four price categories, grouped in the following areas: Dublin city centre, north suburbs, south suburbs and south coast. Although the tourist information offices at Dublin Airport and Suffolk Street have hotel booking facilities, you are advised to book your accommodation well in advance.

Many hotels add a service charge to the quoted price, and some establishments charge more during special events. Be sure to ask what is included in the quoted rates: ask about VAT (government tax), service and breakfast (after a full Irish breakfast you probably won't need lunch). Also ask about special weekend rates and other special offers.

As a basic guide to room prices, we have used the following symbols for a double room with bath or shower (en suite), usually including breakfast, service charge and tax:

€€€€	over 250 euros
€€€	200–250 euros
€€	100–200 euros
€	below 100 euros

CITY CENTRE

Blooms Hotel €–€€ *6 Anglesea Street, Temple Bar, Dublin 2, tel: 671 5622, fax: 671 5997, <www.blooms.ie>.* A convenient modern hotel in the Temple Bar area, Blooms is a decent choice for party-goers, but not for those planning a quiet night. Downstairs is Club M, a busy nightclub.

Brooks Hotel €€€ *Drury Street, Dublin 2, tel: 670 4000, <www.sinnottshotels.com>.* With a great location just a short walk from Dublin's Grafton Street, Brooks is a smart choice in the centre of the city. Rooms are spacious and comfortable and there are plasma screens and DVD players in the newer rooms. 98 rooms.

Buswells Hotel €€ *23–27 Molesworth Street, Dublin 2, tel: 614 6500, fax: 676 2090, <www.quinnhotels.com>*. Centrally located (opposite the National Museums complex) in a former Georgian townhouse, Buswells has an old-world atmosphere and period furnishings. Conference facilities. 69 rooms.

Castle Hotel €–€€ *2–4 Great Denmark Street, Dublin 1, tel: 874 6949, fax: 872 7674, <www.castle-hotel.ie>*. The Castle Hotel consists of three adjacent and tastefully restored Georgian buildings, close to Parnell Square. Authentically restored décor combined with modern comfort. Small conference facilities and parking. 48 rooms.

Central Hotel €–€€ *1–5 Exchequer Street, Dublin 2, tel: 679 7302, fax: 679 7303, <www.centralhotel.ie>*. A comfortable Best Western hotel right beside Temple Bar, decorated and furnished in Victorian style. Dining room, bars, conference facilities. 70 rooms.

Clarence Hotel €€€€ *6–8 Wellington Quay, Dublin 2, tel: 407 0800, fax: 407 0820, <www.theclarence.ie>*. Located in a handsome hotel built in 1852. Recently renovated, each room is uniquely designed in a contemporary manner. Adjacent to Temple Bar and overlooking the River Liffey, it boasts a lovely interior and a fine restaurant, The Tea Rooms. Parking. 43 rooms and 5 suites.

Clarion Hotel €€€ *International Financial Services Centre, Dublin 1, tel: 433 8800, fax: 433 8811, <www.clarionhotelifsc.ie>*. Located along the quays a reasonably short walk from the centre, the Clarion is a good option with contemporary-styled rooms, luxurious suites and serviced apartments for those planning on a longer stay. The hotel also boasts the Sanovitae Health and Fitness Club with gym and swimming pool. 151 rooms and suites, 14 apartments.

Conrad International Dublin €€€€ *Earlsfort Terrace, Dublin 2, tel: 602 8900, fax: 676 5424, <www.conraddublin.com>*. Situated just off St Stephen's Green, this glass construction opposite the National Concert Hall houses one of Ireland's few five-star hotels. The Conrad's gourmet restaurant, traditional pub and elegant tea room could make it difficult to leave. 176 rooms and 16 suites.

Davenport Hotel €€–€€€€ *Merrion Square, Dublin 2, tel: 607 3500, fax: 661 5663, <www.ocallaghanhotels.com>.* The neoclassical style of the impressive facade of this elegant 1860s building is carried over into its vast atrium lobby. Fine-dining restaurant, bar, conference facilities, car park. 103 rooms and 12 suites.

Dylan €€€ *Eastmoreland Place, Dublin 2, tel: 660 3000, fax: 660 3005, <www.dylan.ie>.* A chic and stylish boutique hotel in a quiet location off Baggot Street, about a 15-minute walk from Grafton Street. The individually designed rooms include plasma screens, customised beds and underfloor-heated bathrooms. 43 rooms and suites.

Fitzsimons Hotel €–€€ *21–22 Wellington Quay, Dublin 2, tel: 677 9315, fax: 677 9387, <www.fitzsimonshotel.com>.* If you're coming to Dublin to experience a weekend you'll soon forget (ie a weekend with the lads/lasses) this is the place for you. A huge night club and a bustling loud pub make it an all night affair. By day, the Millennium Bridge provides access to the city's best shopping areas. 28 rooms.

Fitzwilliam Hotel €€€–€€€€ *St Stephen's Green, Dublin 2, tel: 478 7000, fax: 478 7878, www.fitzwilliamhotel.com>.* This up-market modern hotel, located on the Green, has a contemporary and understated elegance. There are views of Dublin from the lovely roof garden. Among its three restaurants, the Michelin-starred Thornton's is one of Dublin's finest. 130 rooms.

Grafton Capital €€ *Stephen's Street Lower, Dublin 2, tel: 648 1100, fax: 648 1122, <www.gtahotels.com>.* This is a good, three-star townhouse-style hotel with a great location that's near to all of Dublin's nightlife scene. Across the road, a string of Dublin's best cafes wait to help you recover from the morning after. 75 rooms.

Gresham Hotel €€–€€€€ *23 Upper O'Connell Street, Dublin 1, tel: 874 6881, fax: 878 7175, <www.gresham-hotels.com>.* One of Dublin's legendary hotels, the Gresham is based in the heart of the city, near the General Post Office. The fine, early 19th-century building, with its marble floors and large rooms offers luxurious accommodation. Two restaurants, two bars. 289 rooms.

Longfields Hotel €–€€ *9–10 Lower Fitzwilliam Street, Dublin 2, tel: 676 1367, fax: 676 1542, <www.longfields.ie>*. Wonderfully located in a splendid Georgian building near Merrion and Fitzwilliam squares, this stylish hotel offers period furnishings, an excellent restaurant and a bar. 26 rooms.

Merrion Hotel €€€€ *Upper Merrion Street, Dublin 2, tel: 603 0600, fax: 603 0700, <www.merrionhotel.com>*. This elegant hotel was created from four Georgian town houses. Its gracious setting, discreet service and beautifully appointed rooms and suites offer an outstanding experience. One of Dublin's notable restaurants, Patrick Guilbaud *(see page 139)* is located here. 122 rooms and 20 suites.

Mont Clare Hotel €€ *Merrion Square, Dublin 2, tel: 607 3800, fax: 661 5663, <www.ocallaghanhotels.ie>*. An attractive hotel with a traditional club-like feel, in a Georgian building on lovely Merrion Square. Convenient for the National Art Gallery, Trinity College and other attractions. Restaurant, bar, car park. 80 rooms.

The Morgan €€–€€€ *10 Fleet Street, Temple Bar, Dublin 2, tel: 643 7000, fax: 643 7060, <www.themorgan.com>*. Simply the most stylish hotel in Temple Bar. You should stay here if you've come to live it up or seduce. You can start in the chic cocktail bar, which also serves tapas. 106 rooms.

Morrison Hotel €€€€ *Lower Ormond Quay, Dublin 1, tel: 887 2400, fax: 878 3185, <www.morrisonhotel.ie>*. A modern building overlooking the River Liffey, this is one of Dublin's most sophisticated hotels. A new spa offering a Turkish bath, aromatherapy massages and other pampering treatments lends a calming ambience, and there's a café, bar and restaurant. 138 rooms.

Number 31 €€–€€€ *31 Leeson Close, Lower Leeson Street, Dublin 2, tel: 676 5011, fax: 676 2929, <www.number31.ie>*. This upscale B&B is a favourite accommodation of regular visitors to Dublin. It features spacious rooms, listed architecture (Georgian or modern, take your pick), a sunken lounge with fireplace, and a fabulous Irish breakfast in the plant-filled conservatory.

The Paramount €–€€€ *Parliament Street, Dublin 2; tel: 417 9900, fax: 417 9904, <www.paramounthotel.ie>.* The Paramount boasts good rooms that have a gentleman's club feel to them with their tobacco-tones and 1930s styling. The location is hard to beat. 70 rooms.

Royal Dublin Hotel €–€€ *O'Connell Street, Dublin 1, tel: 873 3666, fax: 873 3120, <www.royaldublin.com>.* Near Parnell Square, this Best Western hotel is set in one of Dublin's oldest houses dating back to 1752. The public rooms are Georgian, the ensuite bedrooms contemporary. Restaurant and bars, car park. 117 rooms.

Russell Court Hotel €–€€ *21–25 Harcourt Street, Dublin 2, tel: 478 4066, fax: 478 1576 <www.russellcourthotel.ie>.* Two Georgian houses make up this hotel with its Victorian-style décor. A new wing has added six rooms. Restaurant, new nightclub and bars. 52 rooms.

Shelbourne Hotel €€€€ *27 St Stephen's Green, Dublin 2, tel: 663 4500, fax: 661 6006, <www.marriott.co.uk>.* Dublin's most famous hotel is known for its distinction and elegant charm and has recently re-opened after extensive restoration. Some rooms overlook the Green, and all are furnished for style and comfort. A very good restaurant and bar; the lobby is a favourite place for afternoon tea. 188 rooms.

Staunton's on the Green €€ *83 St Stephen's Green South, Dublin 2, tel: 478 2300, fax: 478 2263, <www.stauntonsonthegreen.ie>.* This exclusive Georgian guesthouse, with its splendid high ceilings and windows, overlooks St Stephen's Green in front and the Iveagh Gardens to the rear. The spacious rooms are all en suite. 40 rooms.

Stephen's Green Hotel €€–€€€€ *St Stephen's Green, Dublin 2, tel: 607 3600, fax: 661 5663, <www.ocallaghanhotels.ie>.* This boutique hotel, on the west side of the Green, looks strikingly modern, with a four-storey glass atrium. Restaurant, bar. 75 rooms and suites.

Temple Bar Hotel €€–€€€€ *Fleet Street, Temple Bar, Dublin 2, tel: 677 3333, fax: 677 3088, <www.towerhotelgroup.ie>.* This pleasant hotel is in Temple Bar, near clubs and pubs, and a stone's throw away from Grafton Street. Restaurant and bar. 129 rooms.

Trinity Capital €€–€€€ *Pearse Street, Dublin 2, tel: 648 1000, fax: 648 1010, <www.capital-hotels.com>*. One of several Capital Hotels in the city. Bright, contemporary rooms with cherry wood furnishings. Most rooms have internet access; mini-suites have jacuzzi baths. Restaurant. 82 rooms and suites.

Trinity Lodge €€ *12 South Frederick Street, Dublin 2, tel: 617 0900, fax: 617 0999, <www.trinitylodge.com>*. Tucked along one of the best hidden streets in Dublin you can't get anymore central than this and it's difficult to find a quieter location. Inside the rooms are full of wooden furniture and big, comfy beds. Outside you are next door to one of Dublin's best café society areas. 16 rooms.

The Westbury €€€–€€€€ *Grafton Street, Dublin 2, tel: 679 1122, fax: 679 7078, <www.jurys-dublin-hotels.com>*. A favourite with visiting celebrities, the Westbury is a lush, opulent oasis just off Grafton Street. The Terrace Lounge is a favourite for afternoon tea and the Mandarin Bar is a chic spot to have a pint. 204 rooms and suites.

The Westin €€€€ *Westmoreland Street, Dublin 2, tel: 645 1000, fax: 645 1234, <www.westin.com/dublin>*. The Westin sits on a prime city centre location in a grand historic building that used to be the Allied Irish Bank. It's everything you'd expect from an international 5 star with luxurious guest rooms, fully equipped gym and fine dining. 163 rooms and suites.

Wynn's Hotel €€ *35–39 Lower Abbey Street, Dublin 1, tel: 874 5131, fax: 874 1556, <www.wynnshotel.ie>*. This city centre hotel is just around the corner from the Abbey Theatre. Recently refurbished. Restaurant, bar, conference facilities, parking. 70 rooms.

NORTH OF THE CENTRE

Egan's Guesthouse €–€€ *7–9 Iona Park, Glasnevin, Dublin 9, tel: 830 3611, fax: 830 3312, <www.eganshouse.com>*. Set in a pleasant terrace of Edwardian houses, near the splendid Botanic Gardens, Croke Park and the airport. Car park. 32 rooms.

Park Inn Hotel €€ *Smithfield Village, Dublin 7, tel: 817 3838, fax: 817 3839.* Formerly Chief O'Neill's, the Park Inn is located in the same complex as the Jameson Distillery and the Chimney Viewing Tower. It has smart, bright contemporary rooms. Temple Bar is about a 10-minute walk away, or else you can take the Luas into the city centre.

Regency Airport Hotel €–€€€ *Swords Road, Whitehall, Dublin 9, tel: 837 3544, fax: 836 7121, <www.regencyhotels.com>.* A handy place to stay if you're coming in too late for the fun or too early for the sun. Located between the city and the airport, the rooms are modern and its theme restaurant will feed you well. 210 rooms.

SOUTH OF THE CENTRE

Bewley's Hotel Ballsbridge € *Merrion Road, Ballsbridge, Dublin 4, tel: 668 1111, fax: 668 1999, <www.bewleyshotels.com>.* A spacious and modern hotel behind a restored 1793 facade, with reasonably priced deluxe rooms and suites. Restaurant, bar, car park. 300 rooms.

Burlington Hotel €€–€€€ *Upper Leeson Street, Dublin 4, tel: 660 5222, fax: 660 8496, <www.jurys-dublin-hotels.com>.* A huge and popular hotel, the Burlington has Dublin's largest conference facilities. Restaurants, nightclubs, shops, car park. 500 rooms and 6 suites.

Glenveagh Townhouse € *31 Northumberland Road, Ballsbridge, Dublin 4, tel: 668 4612, fax: 668 4559, <www.glenveagh.com>.* A pleasant Victorian house. Quiet location. Parking. 13 rooms.

Herbert Park Hotel €€–€€€€ *Anglesea Road, Ballsbridge, Dublin 4, tel: 667 2200, <www.herbertparkhotel.ie>.* Stylish, comfortable hotel in the Embassy district. The lounge, bar and restaurant feature furnishings by Irish designers. Rooms have king-size beds. Fitness and business facilities, free car park. 150 rooms and 3 suites.

Lansdowne Hotel €€ *27–29 Pembroke Road, Ballsbridge, Dublin 4, tel: 668 2522, fax: 668 5585, <www.lansdownehotel.com>.* Set back from a tree-lined road in Ballsbridge. Celtic Restaurant, traditional bar, car park. 40 rooms.

Mount Herbert Hotel €–€€ *Herbert Road, Landsdowne, Dublin 4, tel: 668 4321, fax: 660 7077, <www.mountherberthotel.ie>.* A family-run hotel in an extended Victorian building near Lansdowne Road DART. Functional but comfortable ensuite rooms. Children's play area. Restaurant, bar, conference facilities, parking. 180 rooms.

Premier Suites Dublin €€–€€€ *Stephen's Hall, 14–17 Lower Leeson Street, Dublin 2, tel: 638 1111, <www.premiersuitesdublin.com>.* These luxurious serviced apartments are ideal for anyone planning a longer stay. Each suite has a spacious living area with plasma TV, hi-fi and broadband. 27 suites, 7 penthouses.

Raglan Lodge €–€€ *10 Raglan Road, Ballsbridge, Dublin 4, tel: 660 6697, fax: 660 6781.* In a Victorian house dating from 1861, this hotel offers a quiet stay in a peaceful location 10 minutes by bus from Dublin's centre. Award-winning breakfast. Parking. 7 rooms.

Upper Cross House Hotel €€ *26–30 Upper Rathmines Road, Rathmines, Dublin 6, tel: 497 5486, fax: 497 5361, <www.upper crosshousehotel.com>.* Original 19th-century building with modern wing, two miles from the city centre. Comfortable rooms, two restaurants and live music in Mother Reilly's bar. 52 rooms.

SOUTH COAST

Fitzpatrick Castle Hotel €€–€€€ *Killiney Hill Road, Killiney, Co. Dublin, tel: 230 5400, fax: 230 5430, <www.fitzpatrickcastle.com>.* This period residence sits in 3.5 hectares (9 acres) of landscaped gardens and wooded grounds, overlooking Dublin Bay. A courtesy bus (30 minutes) connects it with the city centre. Restaurants, bar, leisure centre, swimming pool, tennis courts and other sports facilities; golf available. Car park. 113 rooms and suites.

Rochestown Hotel €€ *Rochestown Avenue, Dun Laoghaire, Co. Dublin, tel: 285 3555, fax: 285 3914, <www.rochestownlodge.com>.* Rooms have contemporary furnishings, many with views of the Wicklow Mountains. Family rooms are available. Facilities include a gym and health centre. 90 rooms and suites.

Recommended Restaurants

Dublin has a superb range of both traditional Irish and cosmopolitan restaurants. Most offer both fixed price and à la carte menus. A fixed-price three- or four-course meal is often the best value. Meal prices include 12.5 percent government tax (VAT), and a 15 percent service charge is often added to the final bill. Many restaurants offer early or pre-theatre dinners at reduced prices. Look for specials in local publications. Don't forget that most pubs offer good food, and some have dining rooms. Many museums and other attractions have excellent, moderately priced cafés.

As a basic guide, the following symbols give an idea of the price for an average meal for one, including a service charge of 10–15 percent but excluding wine or other drinks:

€€€€	above 30 euros
€€€	20–30 euros
€€	15–25 euros
€	below 15 euros

CITY CENTRE SOUTH

The Bistro €€ *4–5 Castle Market, Dublin 2, tel: 671 5430*. Open Mon noon–10pm, Tue–Wed 9am–10pm, Thur–Sat 9am–11pm, Sun 1–9pm. A friendly, family-run place that draws people back for more of its Italian favourites, located at the popular Castle Market.

Breakfast@Bewley's € *78–79 Grafton Street, Dublin 2, tel: 672 7720*. Open Mon–Fri 8–11.30am, Sat and Sun 9am–noon. Call in for a coffee, the full Irish breakfast or granola, porridge, bagels and scones in this wonderful 1840 building with stained glass decor. In the evening there's a fish restaurant, Mackerel, and the Café Bar Deli upstairs is open noon–10pm (Thur–Sat til 11pm).

Bleu Bistro Moderne €€€ *Joshua House, Dawson Street, Dublin 2, tel: 676 7015, <www.bleu.ie>*. Good ingredients and well-executed dishes make Bleu a favourite amongst Dubliners. There's a lunch, afternoon, pre-theatre and dinner menu making it one of the most flexible spots in town.

Café Bar Deli €–€€ *George's Street, Dublin 2, tel: 677 1646 <www.cafebardeli.ie>.* Open Mon–Sat 12.30–11pm, Sun 2–10pm. Popular café, bar and deli with a reliable selection of pizzas, pastas and salads. Also a branch at Bewleys.

La Cave €€ *28 South Anne Street, Dublin 2, tel: 679 4409, <www. lacavewinebar.com>.* Open Mon–Sat 12.30–11pm, Sun 6–11pm. Dublin's oldest authentic French wine bar, with reasonably priced bistro-style dishes . It's decorated with nostalgic posters and prints, and has an excellent wine list plus a late night menu after 11pm.

The Cedar Tree €€–€€€ *11a St Andrew Street, Dublin 2, tel: 677 2121.* Open Mon–Wed 5.30–11.30pm, Thur–Sat 5.30pm–midnight. The Lebanese food here is authentic and reasonably priced, with good vegetarian options.

Chili Club €€ *1 Anne's Lane, off South Anne Street, Dublin 2, tel: 677 3721.* Open Mon–Sat 12.30–2.30pm and daily 6–11pm. One of the oldest Thai restaurants in Dublin. Good, authentic food served in a small, friendly setting. Vegetarian options on an extensive menu.

Cornucopia € *19 Wicklow Street, Dublin 2, tel: 677 7583.* Open Mon–Sat 8.30am–8pm (Thur until 9pm), Sun noon–7pm. The food is now better than ever at this favourite vegetarian restaurant. A small, informal place, mostly self-service, with table service week-end nights only. Visa is the only credit card accepted.

Dax €€€–€€€€ *23 Upper Pembroke Street, Dublin 2, tel: 676 1494, fax: 676 3287, <www.dax.ie>.* Open Thur and Fri 12.30–2.30pm, 6–11pm, Sat 6–11pm. Dax is worth visiting for its delightful rustic and continental food with a French emphasis. There's a good value early bird tapas style menu from 6–7pm Tue–Thur.

Diep Le Shaker €€€€ *55 Pembroke Lane, Dublin 2, tel: 661 1829, fax: 661 5905, <www.diep.net>.* Open Mon–Thur noon–2.15pm,

Fri 12–11.15pm, Mon–Thur 6.30–10.30pm, Sat 6.30–11.15pm. A smart, upmarket Thai restaurant with contemporary interior design and an authentic menu. It's a little outside the centre of town but it's worth the walk.

Dunne & Crescenzi € *14–16 South Frederick Street, Dublin 2, tel 677 3815, <www.dunneandcrescenzi.com>.* Open Mon–Sat 8.30am–11pm, Sun noon–6pm The tables are packed into this small but pleasantly authentic Italian joint, which focuses more on panini and antipasti than on hot dishes. Everything is well-prepared and big on taste.

L'Ecrivain €€€€ *109a Lower Baggot Street, Dublin 2, tel: 661 1919, <www.lecrivain.com>.* Open Mon–Fri 12.30–2pm and Mon–Sat 7–11pm. One of the best restaurants in the city for new Irish cuisine prepared with a French accent. It is famous for its fish dishes, using same-day catch from all around Ireland.

Eden €€€ *Meeting House Square, Temple Bar, Dublin 2, tel: 670 5372, fax: 670 3330, <www.edenrestaurant.ie>.* Open Mon–Sun 12.30–3pm, Mon–Sat 6–10.30pm, Sun 6–10pm, Sat and Sun brunch noon–3pm. Serving contemporary food with an Irish twist, Eden has a modern, airy interior with outdoor seating on Meeting House Square.

Fallon & Byrne €€€ *11-17 Exchequer Street, Dublin 2; tel: 472 1000, fax: 472 1016, <www.fallonandbyrne.com>.* Fallon & Bryne's beautiful dining room makes it a particularly pleasant place to enjoy lunch or Sunday brunch. It's one of Dublin's newer French restaurants with good service, quality bistro cooking and a fabulous New York-style food store downstairs – if you've any room left.

L'Gueuleton €€–€€€ *Fade Street, Dublin 2; tel: 675 3708.* Open Mon–Sat noon–3pm and 6–10pm. This rustic yet contemporary French restaurant serves up robust dishes with a classic bistro edge. It's hugely popular and has an undeniable charm with its rickety wooden tables and blackboards. No bookings taken.

Gruel € *68A Dame Street, tel: 670 7119.* Open Mon–Wed 10am–9.30pm, Thur–Sat 10am–10.30pm, Sun 10am–9pm. Gruel has a homely atmosphere both in its tiny seating area and in its excellent cooking which specialises in no-nonsense favourites like bangers and mash, sublime roast-in-a-roll and superb homemade cakes.

Good World Restaurant €€ *18 South Great George's Street, Dublin 2, tel: 677 5373.* Open daily 12.30pm–3am. This is a popular place, with the best dim sum in the city. The cooking is good, and less geared to Western tastes than most.

Jaipur €€–€€€ *41–46 South Great Georges Street, Dublin 2, tel: 677 0999.* Open daily 5.30–11.30pm. Fabulous restaurant serving modern Indian food using Irish ingredients such as organic Wicklow lamb, and with a wine list specially chosen to complement the spicy dishes.

La Mère Zou €€€€ *22 St Stephen's Green, Dublin 2, tel: 661 6669, <www.lamerezou.ie>.* Open Mon–Fri 12.30–2.30pm and 6–10.30pm, until 11pm Fri–Sat and 9.30pm Sun. A beguiling French-Belgian restaurant with a country air, downstairs on the north side of the Green. Very good food, delicious desserts and friendly service.

The Mermaid Café *69-70 Dame Street, tel: 670 8236, <www.mermaid.ie>.* Open Mon–Sat 12.30–2pm, 6–11pm, Sun noon–3.30pm, 6–9pm. Upmarket sister to Gruel Café, the Mermaid is an elegant, innovative restaurant. Expect a wide variety of France-meets-East Coast America-style dishes with a great selection of super fresh fish. Sunday brunch is a favourite with Dubliners.

Patrick Guilbaud €€€€ *21 Upper Merrion Street, Dublin 4, tel: 676 4192, <www.restaurantpatrickguilbaud.ie>.* Open Tue–Sat 12.30–2.15pm and 7.30–10.15pm. This is Dublin's finest French restaurant, with commensurate prices. In an elegant 18th-century townhouse adjoining the Merrion Hotel.

Roly's Bistro €€€ *7 Ballsbridge Terrace, Dublin 4, tel: 668 0623, <www.rolysbistro.ie>.* Open noon–2.45pm and 5.30–9.45pm. Attractive bistro restaurant on two floors, with imaginative and well-presented menus, usually focused around classic fish and meat dishes. Good service and a lively atmosphere.

Saba €€€ *26-28 Clarendon Street, Dublin 2, tel: 679 2000, 679 2002, <www.sabadublin.com>.* Open Mon–Sun noon–til late. A popular Thai eatery known for its authentic menu and contemporary interior. Features wok-based dishes, salads, noodles and curries.

Steps of Rome €€ *1 Chatham Court, Dublin 2, tel: 670 5630.* Open Mon–Sat noon–11pm, Sun 1–10pm. This tiny restaurant has great pizza; the best in Dublin. The service is friendly, and you can take away. Get there early – there are only a few tables. No credit cards.

Town Bar and Grill €€€–€€€€ *21 Kildare Street, Dublin 2; tel: 662 4724, fax: 662 3857, <www.townbarandgrill.com>.* Open Mon–Sat noon–11pm, Sun noon–10pm. Regarded as one of Dublin's best restaurants serving sophisticated trattoria-style Italian dishes.

Unicorn 12B €€€–€€€€ *Merrion Court, Merrion Row, Dublin 2, tel: 676 2812.* Open Mon–Sat 12.30–4.30pm, 6–11pm. Popular with Dublin's media set, the Unicorn comes into its own in the summer when the doors open out onto a pretty courtyard. The regional Italian food is well-executed and the huge buffet lunches are a treat.

Venu Brasserie €€–€€€ *Anne's Lane, Dublin 2, tel: 670 6755 Open Mon–Sun noon–11pm.* Roomy French brasserie with cool, plain décor offering great quality food. Expect classic French brasserie dishes.

Yamamori Noodles €€–€€€ *71 South Great George's Street, Dublin 2, tel: 475 5001.* Open daily from 12.30pm, last orders at 11.30pm. Japanese restaurant and a good choice for noodles in Dublin. The clientele is predominantly cool.

OLD TOWN/LIBERTIES

Leo Burdock's € *2 Werburgh Street, Dublin 8, tel: 454 0306.* Open Mon–Sat noon–midnight, Sun 4pm–midnight. Dublin's most famous chippy, established in 1913, has no indoor seating but serves the freshest, most delicious fish and chips to take away. Opposite Christchurch Cathedral.

Les Frères Jacques €€€€ *74 Dame Street, Dublin 2, tel: 679 4555, <www.lesfreresjacques.com>.* Open Mon–Fri 12.30–2.30pm, and 7.30–10.30pm, Sat 7.15–11pm. Next to the Olympia Theatre, this small restaurant offers French cuisine in a pleasant, relaxed setting.

TEMPLE BAR

Elephant and Castle €–€€ *18 Temple Bar, Dublin 2, tel: 679 3121, <www.elephantandcastle.com>.* Open Mon–Fri 8.30am–noon, Sat 10am–noon, Sun 10am–4.30pm. Good food and reasonable prices have assured the continuing popularity of this informal place. Come here for burgers and salads as well as the famous spicy chicken wings.

Gallagher's Boxty House €–€€ *20–21 Temple Bar, Dublin 2, tel: 677 2762, <www.boxtyhouse.ie>.* Open daily noon–11pm. Boxty is an old Irish dish: potato pancakes stuffed with a variety of fillings (including vegetarian), served at long tables to traditional Irish background music; a must stop for every tourist.

CITY CENTRE NORTH

Chapter One Restaurant €€€€ *18–19 Parnell Square, Dublin 1, tel: 873 2266, <www.chapteronerestaurant.com>.* Open Tue–Fri 12.30–2pm, Tue–Sat 6–11pm. In the basement of the Dublin Writers Museum, this is one of the city's best, with excellent modern Irish dishes accompanied by fine wines.

101 Talbot €€€ *100–102 Talbot Street (Upstairs), Dublin 1, tel: 874 5011.* Open Tue–Sat 5–11pm. Don't be put off by the dingy neighbourhood – this popular restaurant serves excellent international food in generous portions. The staff are friendly, prices reasonable and there is a good wine list.

Rhodes D7 €€€–€€€€ *The Capel Building, Marys Abbey, Dublin 7, tel: 804 4444, fax: 804 4445, <www.rhodesd7.com>.* Open Mon noon–4pm, Tue–Sat noon–10pm. This is Michelin-starred British chef Gary Rhodes' first venture in Ireland. Mezzanine floor, outdoor heated eating area and an extensive menu.

SOUTH SUBURBS

La Finezza €€€ *Over Kiely's, 22–24 Donnybrook Road, Dublin 4, tel: 283 7166.* Open Mon–Sat 5–11pm, Sun 4–9.30pm. In the heart of Donnybrook village, this restaurant has a convivial atmosphere. The food offers vegetarian choices but relies on seafood and pasta.

O'Connells in Ballsbridge €€€€ *Merrion Road, Ballsbridge, Dublin 4, tel: 647 3304, fax: 647 3398, <www.oconnellsballsbridge. com>.* Open Mon–Sat 12.30–2.30pm, Sun 12.30–3pm; Mon–Sat 6–10.30pm, Sun 6–9.30pm. Located in the Bewley's Hotel on Merrion Road, the food here is modern and utilises the very best in fresh Irish ingredients. Expect delicious roast and fresh seafood.

Poulots €€€€ *Mulberry Gardens, Donnybrook, Dublin 4, tel: 269 3300, <www.poulots.ie>.* Open Tue–Fri 12.30–2.30pm and Tue–Sat 7–10.30pm. The elegant, high-ceilinged dining room complements the modern style and clean lines of Jean-Michel Poulot's gourmet dishes. The superb cuisine is accompanied by an extensive wine list.

OUTSIDE DUBLIN

Caviston's €€€–€€€€ *Sandycove, County Dublin, tel: 280 9245, <www.cavistons.com>.* Open Tue–Fri, lunch is over three sittings: noon–1.30pm, 1.30–3pm and 3pm–close. This tiny fish-restaurant has gained an excellent reputation thanks to its delectable seafood dishes.

Cruzzo Bar & Restaurant €€€€ *Marina Village, Malahide, County Dublin, tel: 845 0599, fax: 845 0602, <www.cruzzo.ie>.* Open Mon–Fri noon–2.30pm and 6–10pm, Sat 5.30–10.30pm, Sun 12.30–3.15pm and 6.30–9.30pm. Situated in Malahide marina, the bar and restaurant are built on a platform over the water. Original paintings adorn the walls; fresh seafood (of course) fills the plates.

Vermilion Indian Fusion Cuisine €€ *94–96 Terenure Road North, Dublin 6W, tel: 499 1400, <www.vermilion.ie>.* Open daily 5.30pm–late, Sun from 1.30pm. The designers have fused hip European style with masala, with great success.

INDEX

Berlitz pocket guide
Dublin

Seventh Edition 2008
Written by Alice Fellows
Updated by Max Media
Principal photographer: Glyn Genin
Series Editor: Tony Halliday

Photography credits
Glyn Genin 9, 11, 14, 20, 22, 24, 25, 33, 34, 39,
40, 45, 46, 47, 48, 49, 50, 51, 53, 54, 57, 59, 62,
63, 67, 76, 82, 84, 85, 89, 95, 99, 100; Richard
Nowitz 6, 27, 30, 41, 44, 72, 79, 90, 93, 103;
Doug Plummer 36, 43, 52, 55, 58, 60, 65, 75, 77;
Geray Sweeney 29, 69, 71; Marcus Wilson-
Smith 96; Bridgeman Art Library 16; Robert
Harding Picture Library Limited/Alamy 86;
Ripani Massimo/SIME-4Corners Images 94;
Popperfoto/Alamy 19; age photostock/
SuperStock 79.

Cover picture: Mark Thomas/Getty Images

Contact us

At Berlitz we strive to keep our guides as
accurate and up to date as possible, but if you
find anything that has changed, or if you have
any suggestions on ways to improve this guide,
then we would be delighted to hear from you.

Berlitz Publishing, PO Box 7910,
London SE1 1WE, England.
fax: (44) 20 7403 0290
email: berlitz@apaguide.co.uk
www.berlitzpublishing.com